Advanced Introduction to U.S. Data Privacy Law

Elgar Advanced Introductions are stimulating and thoughtful introductions to major fields in the social sciences, business and law, expertly written by the world's leading scholars. Designed to be accessible yet rigorous, they offer concise and lucid surveys of the substantive and policy issues associated with discrete subject areas.

The aims of the series are two-fold: to pinpoint essential principles of a particular field, and to offer insights that stimulate critical thinking. By distilling the vast and often technical corpus of information on the subject into a concise and meaningful form, the books serve as accessible introductions for undergraduate and graduate students coming to the subject for the first time. Importantly, they also develop well-informed, nuanced critiques of the field that will challenge and extend the understanding of advanced students, scholars and policy-makers.

For a full list of titles in the series please see the back of the book. This is also available on https://www.elgaronline.com/ and https://www.advancedintros.com/ for Elgar Advanced Introduction in Law.

Advanced Introduction to

U.S. Data Privacy Law

ARI EZRA WALDMAN

Professor of Law, University of California, Irvine School of Law, USA

Elgar Advanced Introductions

 Edward Elgar
PUBLISHING

Cheltenham, UK • Northampton, MA, USA

Published by
Edward Elgar Publishing Limited
The Lypiatts
15 Lansdown Road
Cheltenham
Glos GL50 2JA
UK

Edward Elgar Publishing, Inc.
William Pratt House
9 Dewey Court
Northampton
Massachusetts 01060
USA

A catalogue record for this book
is available from the British Library

Library of Congress Control Number: 2023943176

This book is available electronically on Elgar Advanced Introductions: Law
www.advancedintros.com

Printed on elemental chlorine free (ECF)
recycled paper containing 30% Post-Consumer Waste

ISBN 978 1 80088 143 3 (cased)
ISBN 978 1 80088 145 7 (paperback)
ISBN 978 1 80088 144 0 (eBook)
Printed and bound in the USA

Contents

Preface

Many people outside the legal academy wonder if what I do really matters. They don't mean law teaching. They mean privacy. "Do we even have privacy anymore?" they say. I used to get frustrated. Now I have a better response: "You realize that's exactly what tech companies want you to think, right?"

It's true. Companies that profit off surveilling our every move want us to think that privacy is gone. They want to normalize data extraction. More than that; they want us to think that a robust form of privacy—the kind that enables human flourishing—cannot exist today if we want engaging and tailored social media or access to online commerce or the frictionless ease of Wi-Fi-connected devices. These companies have worked hard and have become quite adept at making protecting our privacy so difficult and so incomplete that we just give up.

But blaming the information industry only goes so far. Technology companies exist within a political economy in which the means of producing profit is constant surveillance. That kind of economy is the creation of law.

This book helps explain the law's role in both commercial surveillance and privacy nihilism. And, spoilers, the law's role is significant and, I would argue, intentional. In short, privacy law in the U.S. has evolved, but it has always been in service of corporate power and purposely so. This argument runs counter to a lot of what we're hearing in the news and from many scholars. People say privacy law is getting stronger. They point to record fines and new investigations and scores of new proposals for comprehensive privacy legislation. They see those proposals doing much more than simply requiring privacy policies and consent buttons.

But as with most cursory analyses that never go below the surface or look under the hood, the story is far more complicated. Yes, privacy law in the U.S. has changed, but it has changed in a way that lends itself conveniently and necessarily to cooptation by the very people, organizations, and companies that it is supposed to regulate. In fact, I argue that this new privacy law is even worse: It creates a false halo of legitimacy for data extractive behavior in a way that mere notice and choice could not. In other words, U.S. privacy law is moving, but it's not moving forward.

This book describes where U.S. privacy law has been, where it is going, and where it needs to go in the future. As befits the book series, it is both "advanced" and an "introduction," which is a difficult line to walk. This "introduction" to U.S. privacy law is "advanced" in the sense that I assume some basic knowledge of law, privacy, and the world in which we live. But I will make my argument—that privacy law in the U.S. has gone through two "waves" that disempower users and facilitate data extraction in different ways—accessible to any readers who are engaged, interested, and keen to learn more. You don't need any background in technology to read and learn from this book. Nor must you be a law student, a law professor, a lawyer, or know any law students, law professors, or lawyers. You just need to be interested in privacy.

Parts of this book are based on or come directly from some of my previously published scholarship, including: "Privacy's Rights Trap," an essay in Volume 117 of the *Northwestern University Law Review Online*, published in 2022; "Privacy, Practice, and Performance," an article in Volume 110 of the *California Law Review*, also published in 2022; "The New Privacy Law," an essay in Volume 55 of the *U.C. Davis Law Review Online*, published in 2021; "Outsourcing Privacy," an essay in Volume 96 of the *Notre Dame Law Review Reflection*, also published in 2021; "Privacy Law's False Promise," an article in Volume 97 of the *Washington University Law Review*, published in 2020; "Privacy, Notice, and Design," an article in Volume 21 of the *Stanford Technology Law Review*, published in 2018; and *Privacy as Trust: Information Privacy for an Information Age*, published by Cambridge University Press in 2018. Many of the concepts discussed throughout this text are treated in more exciting and rich detail in my book, *Industry Unbound: The Inside Story of Privacy, Data, and Corporate Power*, published in 2021 by Cambridge University Press. That book is based on years of field work inside technology companies and what I learned during that research and writing process is why I remain skeptical that mediocre, reformist tweaks to the law will ever be enough to rein in extractive business models at the very core of the information industry.

It is a privilege to be asked to write this text alongside so many well-known and accomplished scholars in this series. To be trusted with that responsibility is an honor, and one I owe to the community of privacy scholars that have welcomed, taught, and guided me. I dedicate this book to them, to my mentors, and specifically to those mentors who have become my friends: Danielle Keats Citron, Julie E. Cohen, Ryan Calo, Woody Hartzog, Neil M. Richards, Frank Pasquale, Paul Schwartz, Paul Ohm, and Daniel J. Solove. I would also like to dedicate this book to a mentor and friend that we lost decades too soon, the late Joel R. Reidenberg.

1 Introduction to U.S. data privacy law

This book is both timely and maybe already a little outdated. It's timely because the information age poses unique and vexing challenges to our privacy. At the same time, it's also probably a little outdated because while you're reading this sentence, legislators and their staff experts are discussing, crafting, and introducing new privacy laws and technology companies are building and marketing new ways to extract data for profit. It is the challenge of law and technology scholarship to remain evergreen in a fast-changing field. We inevitably fail, at least a little bit. To minimize those failures, this book tries to conceptualize, in broad strokes, where United States privacy law has been, where it is, and where it is going. It is not a simple summary of this or that piece of legislation, although we will talk about laws like the Children's Online Privacy Protection Act (COPPA) and the Health Insurance Portability and Accountability Act (HIPAA). You may find yourself reading this in different stages of the evolution of privacy governance. But I doubt you'll find the book irrelevant or antiquated. At least, I hope not. And if you do, know that I tried my best.

In the United States, there are privacy rules that govern what private individuals can do with information about us. That's privacy tort law. There are also rules that constrain or enable government collection of information. That's constitutional information privacy, the Fourth Amendment, and federal and state surveillance law. And there are privacy rules that are supposed to regulate what corporate actors—from Google to the newest startup—can do with data they gather from individuals. That's consumer privacy law, and it includes tort law, contract law, statutes, and agency regulations. These rules seem to be changing fast, but as we shall see, they all pretty much look the same when you peel back the outer layers of the onion. There are other privacy regimes, of course; three is already way too many for this little book and those three categories are already oversimplifications of a more complex overlapping regime. Therefore, although we will talk a little bit about tort, contract, and constitutional law, we'll focus most on the privacy rules that apply to data-intensive industries that collect information from our daily lives in the information age.

The book makes three arguments—one descriptive, one normative, and one prescriptive. The descriptive argument is that we can divide United States consumer privacy law into "waves". The first wave coincided with the mass popularization of the Internet and the original dot com boom of the 1990s, but its origins can be found decades earlier. This wave, which is described in Part I, is *self-regulatory*. We find ourselves in privacy's second wave today, several years after a new generation of privacy laws and regulators introduced impact assessments, audits, and new privacy offices as forms of governance. This wave, which is described in Part II, reflects the decades-long trend toward so-called "new" or "collab-orative" governance,[1] and although it retains many of the features of self-regulation, it is decidedly *managerial*.

This leads to the book's normative argument—namely, that although the second wave is certainly different than the first, it is in many ways less effective than even self-regulation at protecting privacy because its model—individual rights and corporate procedural compliance—provides a sheen of legitimacy to data-extractive behavior. In other words, self-regulation was so obviously subject to capture and so obviously weak and ineffective that it is hard to imagine anyone legitimately thinking posting a privacy policy on the Internet was any kind of regulation at all. But the addition of new rights and many new compliance obligations makes it seem like technology companies have a lot of regulations limiting what they can do with our data. It turns out, however, that for a whole host of reasons we will discuss, this approach to privacy law has done

---

[1]   New governance (subset of it known as collaborative governance) will be more fully detailed below, but is described in the following canonical arti-cles: Jody Freeman, *Collaborative Governance in the Administrative State*, 45 U.C.L.A. L. REV. 1 (1997); Kenneth A. Bamberger, *Regulation as Delegation: Private Firms, Decisionmaking, and Accountability in the Administrative State*, 56 DUKE L.J. 377, 385-92 (2006); Jody Freeman, *The Private Role in Public Governance*, 75 N.Y.U. L. REV. 543 (2000); Orly Lobel, *The Renew Deal: The Fall of Regulation and the Rise of Governance in Contemporary Legal Thought*, 89 MINN. L. REV. 342 (2004).

more harm than good. This normative argument is made throughout Parts I and II.

Given this problem, the book ends with its prescriptive argument. We need a third wave of privacy law, the beginnings of which are outlined in Part III. The third wave is our potential and our future. We may be seeing the first hints of it in recent approaches to privacy and artificial intelligence, including civil rights protections, disgorgement of ill-gotten gains, and bans on facial recognition. But these are just traces of what could be. The third wave could sweep aside rather than replicate managerial privacy law, but only if we can identify the failures of the first and second waves. By the end of this book, I will propose what a post-managerial, substantive consumer privacy law could look like if we let ourselves imagine a better, more autonomous, and less extractive world.

Here is what to expect from this book.

In Part I, we will ask: *Where has privacy law been?* Remarkable at it may seem, the Federal Trade Commission (FTC), the de facto privacy regulator in the U.S., initially disclaimed any interest in regulating technology companies' data extraction practices. When companies started posting privacy policies, the FTC eventually decided to enforce the promises those polices made. Over time, consumer privacy law in the U.S. became a combination of sector-specific federal statutes, FTC consent decrees, and a default transparency requirement known as notice-and-consent.[2] Among other practices, industry wrote and posted privacy policies, individuals were expected to read them, and regulators enforced the promises companies made themselves.[3] This is the regime of click-to-agree, opt-out consents, and long legalese privacy notices.[4] Governance was self-regulatory and based on the idea that the best government involve-

---

[2] *See* Daniel J. Solove and Woodrow Hartzog, *The FTC and the New Common Law of Privacy*, 114 COLUM. L. REV. 583, 600-06, 628-30 (2011).

[3] Various state laws required specific notices. *See, e.g.*, California Online Privacy Protection Act (CalOPPA), CAL. BUS. & PROF. CODE § 22575 (requiring any commercial websites or online services collecting information on California residents to "conspicuously" display a privacy policy with specific details); Delaware Online Privacy and Protection Act, DEL. CODE ANN. § 1205(c) (stating similar requirements as CalOPPA).

[4] *See* Joel R. Reidenberg et al., *Privacy Harms and the Effectiveness of the Notice and Choice Framework*, 11 I/S: J. L. & POL'Y FOR INFO. SOC'Y 485,

ment in private business is the least government involved in private business. That was privacy law's first wave.

This first wave was premised on four long-standing assumptions: (1) that we can adequately process and understand notices about what others will do with our data, (2) that our decision-making is rational, (3) that consent is the same thing as making a real choice, and (4) that consent at scale is empowering. These assumptions are still deeply embedded in how we think about privacy in the U.S.; their fingerprints are everywhere. However, none of those assumptions have any basis in reality. They are fictions invented to prop up a mostly self-regulatory regime that empowers technology companies at our expense.

The first wave empowered industry because real choice is illusory. The work necessary to create even the tiniest semblance of control over data is beyond most people's capabilities. There are too many websites, too many consent toggles, too many cookies, and too many options at the same time that there are too few search, social media, and digital platform companies. The first wave's decision to focus on consent may sound empowering to those doing the consenting. But the reality is entirely different.

Part II asks: *Where is privacy law now?* Notice-and-consent has not disappeared. But privacy law is changing. Its second wave requires more than just a privacy policy and a button to click "Agree". It asks more of industry than merely writing, posting, and adhering to a privacy policy that no one reads. It adds practices like completing privacy impact assessments ("PIAs"), hiring chief privacy officers ("CPOs") and staffs, conducting audits, writing and adhering to industry codes of conduct, self-certifying compliance, keeping records and paper trails, automating compliance, and developing internal processes for adjudicating customer rights. But those differences, though notable, neither materially shift privacy law's political economy nor meaningfully limit the information economy's data-extractive business model. Different, yes; substantive, no.

490-96 (2015) (summarizing broad critiques of the notice-and-consent framework).

The press and many privacy scholars think privacy law is getting stronger, the requirements getting stricter, and the potential impact getting bigger.[5] Privacy law is indeed changing—from a first wave of "notice-and-consent" to a second wave of individual rights and compliance obligations—but, as we will see, it isn't getting any stronger. Privacy law has been a gift to industry from the beginning. Its wrapping paper is changing; maybe the bow is a little flashier. But it's still a gift. From the beginning, privacy law put the onus of protecting privacy on you and me, and we are simply incapable of shouldering that burden. There are too many choices and too many privacy policies; we lack the cognitive ability to exercise our privacy at that scale. And even if we could read and understand privacy policies and translate our comprehension into informed consent, privacy law's focus on the individual misses how today's Internet's business model— one based on targeted behavioral advertising algorithmically determined based on data extracted from our every move—actually functions. Privacy law to date is also agnostic as to power, failing to consider the unique risks faced by marginalized populations.

The supposedly stronger second wave makes these same mistakes while also giving a sheen of legitimacy to a manipulative business model left almost entirely untouched. Individual rights of control—including the right to access, correct, delete, and opt out—at the heart of second wave privacy law double down on privacy self-management.[6] Mandates like the "comprehensive privacy program" clause in FTC consent decrees are mere symbols of compliance that make it seem like companies are taking privacy seriously when all they're doing is putting a new façade on a shack. In short, privacy law has become managerialized, where symbols stand in for actual privacy protections.

What do I mean by managerialization? Managerialism, in brief, refers to a set of practices that is supposedly "informed by best practices in private-sector management."[7] Managerialism is also an ideology—

[5]   E.g., Meg Leta Jones and Margot E. Kaminski, *An American's Guide to the GDPR*, 98 DENV. L. REV. 93 (2020); William McGeveran, *Friending the Privacy Regulators*, 58 ARIZ. L. REV. 959, 963 (2016).

[6]   Daniel J. Solove, *Introduction: Privacy Self-Management and the Consent Dilemma*, 126 HARV. L. REV. 1880 (2013).

[7]   Julie E. Cohen and Ari Ezra Waldman, *Forward: Framing Regulatory Managerialism as an Object of Study and Strategic Displacement*, 86 L. & CONTEMP. PROBS. (forthcoming 2023).

namely, the belief that private-sector practices are the best way to organize and oversee economic production. It involves public-private partnerships, procedural informality, reliance on a cadre of compliance professionals, the valorization of efficiency, and other practices and orientations that privilege private sector innovation, profit, and growth over other values.[8]

Privacy law is not the only area of law that has been managerialized. In environmental law, financial law, anti-discrimination law, and a host of other areas, procedural informality and meaningless paperwork are standing in for real change. But an impact assessment is no replacement for public governance; filling out a form is not protecting privacy. And yet this is what passes for regulation in the second wave.

The narrative of privacy law has not ended. Its future has not been written. Therefore, Part III asks: *Where does privacy law go from here?* This is the critical question. Privacy law is at a crossroads. The second wave is arguably reifying mistakes that have contributed to ubiquitous commodification and corporate surveillance. But we still have the chance to advise lawmakers to chart a new path. Now is the time to understand where we have been, where we are, and where we need to go if we want to safeguard any semblance of privacy in the information age. We need a third wave of privacy law, one that will bring real accountability after the managerial turn. This "wave" language, by the way, isn't my invention. I'm borrowing from dynamic scholarship in feminism, whose own "third wave" put the intersectional emancipation of women at its core.[9] Maybe feminism's third wave can teach us a little something about privacy law's to-do list.

To that end, this final part details a few principles to keep in mind when building new forms of privacy governance. It doesn't dive into the details of statutory language or proposal minutiae; you may be reading this book 20 years after publication and new ideas have probably come along.

8   JULIE E. COHEN, BETWEEN TRUTH AND POWER: THE LEGAL CONSTRUCTIONS OF INFORMATIONAL CAPITALISM (2019).
9   *See, e.g.*, Aya Gruber, *Neofeminism*, 50 HOUS. L. REV. 1325, 1331-45, 1372-90 (2013) (analyzing second wave "orthodoxies" and providing a third wave critique); Martha Minow, *Introduction: Finding Our Paradoxes, Affirming Our Beyond*, 24 HARV. C.R.-C.L. L. REV. 1, 1-3 (1989) (describing three "stage[s]" of feminism).

Instead, it describes in broad strokes what a third wave of privacy law has to do and how it can do it. This Part will talk about how we can reclaim public governance traditions while building new forms of democratic accountability for the information industry. Some of the proposals may strike you as sensible and obvious; for example, the FTC needs an enormous infusion of money, personnel, and explicit authorization to do its job better. Other ideas may come off as radical, but they are no less necessary; for example, I think the only way we will be able to protect privacy in an information, surveillance-based economy is with robust public and non-profit options that put privacy first and can withstand market demands for more and more data. For decades, we have been unable to imagine what real regulation of runaway commercial surveillance can look like. I would like to start us thinking again. With these principles in mind, privacy law's third wave can accomplish what the first and second waves have not even tried—namely, shifting the balance of power in informational capitalism from data-extractive industries to the people.

A few other notes before we begin. First, because I am an academic, this book has footnotes. They will cite to scholarship, laws, and articles in the press. Just like this book is meant to be accessible to all, everything cited is accessible, as well. Some sources may require more work than others, but anyone who might want to read this short text—students, practitioners, everyone interested in privacy—will be able.

Second, because this book is small—you may finish it on a short train ride or while you wait for an actual human customer service representative on the phone—it is necessarily underinclusive. Entire fields of law are given short shrift; canonical scholarship may be left out. It does not cover more than 100 years of development of privacy tort law. Nor does it focus much at all on the rules that navigate government collection of data. I ask that you approach this book as less a comprehensive review of every corner of the privacy world than a brief survey highlighting some of the important aspects of the legal regime governing technology companies' collection, sharing, and use of consumer and user data in the U.S.

Third, because this book has one author, it reflects one person's perspective, which has been developed over time from the entire world of my personal and professional experiences. I have experienced data- and disclosure-related harms, one among them being nonconsensual pornography. I am a member of a community—the LGBTQ+ community—that faces unique risks if privacy law remains as weak as it is today. I'm also a law professor, not a privacy professional, privacy lawyer, or technology designer. I am not constrained by perceptions of what is and instead focus on what can be. That said, I cannot speak for all survivors of cyberabuse, for all queer people, or for all academics. I recognize the limitations of my experiences and perspective. Therefore, although I make arguments throughout this book that tell a story of privacy law as an enabler of corporate power, I will also cite to the work of others who may disagree with me. Their perspective is important, too, especially as you develop your own views and, with any luck, take a critical eye to what you read.

Fourth and finally, because this book is an introduction to a large and growing area of law with many scholars and practitioners, some of the arguments you will read in this book have been echoed by others and, therefore, could be considered mainstream and accepted by many or even most scholars. For example, I think a lot of people, maybe with the exception of any industry mouthpiece, think that notice-and-consent is, at the very least, insufficient. At the same time, because one person is writing this, some of the arguments you will read are, at the moment, pretty radical. I don't think consent should be a means for corporate collection of data at scale — ever. Many other scholars believe that consent still has some role to play. I will argue later in this book at privacy laws that are based on individual rights of control—rights of access, correction, deletion, and so forth—do more harm than good. Many scholars and advocates think those laws are better than nothing. I will make the arguments and you can decide for yourself.

With those caveats, let's begin. After this Introduction, Part I focuses on where we have been. Chapter 2 summaries the origins, justifications, and on-the-ground practices of the early privacy law regimes known as "notice-and-consent". Chapter 3 critiques "notice-and-consent" by focusing on its faulty assumptions. Part II then describes where we are now—namely, in commercial privacy law's second wave. Chapter 4 describes the two sides to the second wave: individual privacy rights of control—such as rights to access the information companies have us, rights to delete that information, and rights to correct it, among others— and internal structures of compliance—privacy offices and staffs, impact assessments, and audits, among others. Chapters 5 and 6 demonstrate the weaknesses of the rights/compliance model, with Chapter 5 homing in on critiques of individual rights as effective privacy governance and Chapter

6 critiquing the second wave practice of relying on procedural compliance structures entirely under the control of technology companies themselves. Part III then looks ahead by considering what a third wave of privacy law in the U.S. could look like. I conclude with optimism about that future, so let's work together to make it all the way through.

PART I

PRIVACY LAW'S FIRST WAVE

2   The first wave of notice-and-consent

Privacy law is not new. As Samuel Warren and Louis Brandeis argued in "The Right to Privacy," their canonical 1890 article in the *Harvard Law Review*, the notion that the law can protect "inviolate personality" is as old as the common law.[1] Warren and Brandeis were concerned about the potential for new technologies—in their case, the new, instantaneous camera—to invade the "sacred precincts" of other people's lives.[2] They saw an overeager press using new technology to take pictures from far away, write salacious stories about private lives, and open up the lifestyles of the wealthy to public scrutiny. They argued that the common law of torts offered a perfect way of protecting their privacy.

Warren's and Brandeis's concern about privacy focused mostly on elites. They were chiefly concerned about the privacy of the wealthy, so that people like them could enjoy life behind their high hedges and in their spacious homes in leafy neighborhoods.[3] But their theories and rhetoric, particularly about the ways in which technology can create new means of surveillance, apply to everyone.

The information economy brings with it new technologies and institutions that threaten to erode our privacy. In particular, the information age business model in which data about consumers is extracted, processed by machine learning, and churned out in the form of targeted advertisements and predictive algorithms transforms the minutiae of daily life

---

[1]   Samuel Warren and Louis Brandeis, *The Right to Privacy*, 4 HARV. L. REV. 193, 211 (1890).

[2]   *Id.* at 195.

[3]   ROBERT E. SMITH, BEN FRANKLIN'S WEBSITE 125, 135-36 (2000); Neil M. Richards, *The Puzzle of Brandeis, Privacy, and Speech*, 63 VAND. L. REV. 1295, 1304 (2010).

into grist for profit. The result is a form of capitalism based on constant surveillance. But informational capitalism is a legal construct, not simply an economic one.[4] As we will see, consumer privacy law's first attempt at regulating the data-extractive economy was to barely regulate it all. In short, Internet platforms could set their own rules and collect and use as much data as they wanted as long as the company posted a privacy policy. That way, users could know what would happen with their data, equipping them to make choices about which website to use. Unfortunately, this "notice-and-consent" approach to privacy law only further empowered technology companies.

2.1   Origins of notice-and-consent

The first wave of consumer privacy law in the United States started with the popularization of the World Wide Web. For the first time, millions of people were logging into a network of computers and access was being provided by private, for-profit intermediaries like America Online, Netscape, and Compuserve. Widespread Internet use generated popular concerns about privacy and what was then called Personally Identifiable Information, or PII (things like Social Security Numbers, financial records, and health and medical information). Soon, people starting buying things online, which meant entering in their credit card numbers. The Internet offered a host of opportunities to collect data about billions of people.

At the time, however, online data was collected in a regulatory void. There were no generally applicable laws in the U.S. that limited what websites could do with our information. So individuals and groups of plaintiffs tried to shoehorn old law into new dynamics. For example, when they realized that American Express was selling their purchase histories and other personal data for profit, cardholders sued the company using the common law tort of invasion of privacy.[5] It didn't work. In *Dwyer v. American Express*, an Illinois appellate court said, among other things, that by using an American Express card, cardholders voluntarily gave up

---

[4]   JULIE E. COHEN, BETWEEN TRUTH AND POWER: LEGAL CONSTRUCTIONS OF INFORMATIONAL CAPITALISM 3 (2019).

[5]   Dwyer v. Am. Express Co., 652 N.E.2d 1351 (Ill. App. Ct. 1995).

their information to the company. When another group of Internet users learned about cookies—small tracking files downloaded onto our computers so websites remember us when we return—they turned to statutes originally intended to regulate wiretapping.[6] They argued that the online advertising company DoubleClick was intercepting and storing their information without their consent. Again, they failed. A federal court in *In re DoubleClick, Inc. Privacy Litigation* said that the websites that used DoubleClick's advertising technology consented to the data collection, and that was enough.

2.2   What is notice-and-consent?

When policymakers started paying attention to consumer privacy issues during the early years of the Clinton Administration, early Internet companies turned to data use notices as a way to stave off more aggressive regulation.[7] The FTC, the U.S.'s consumer protection regulator, initially disclaimed any interest in monitoring, let alone regulating, these notices and the companies' underlying data-extractive practices.[8] But the Commission couldn't ignore the Internet for too long. Within a few years, it started enforcing the promises companies made in their notices pursuant to its authority in Section 5 of the Federal Trade Commission Act, which prohibits "unfair or deceptive acts or practices in or affecting commerce."[9] Since then, what we now know as privacy policies have become ubiquitous.

The idea was simple: Internet companies would post a notice describing all the ways they collected, used, and processed consumer information, and the terms under which that information would be shared, sold, or disseminated to others. Using these detailed notices, consumers could decide for themselves if they wanted to use a particular website. They could then consent to the data collection and use by using the website

---

6   *In re* DoubleClick, Inc. Privacy Litigation, 154 F. Supp. 2d 497, 511 (S.D.N.Y. 2001).

7   Daniel J. Solove and Woodrow Hartzog, *The FTC and the New Common Law of Privacy*, 114 Colum. L. Rev. 583, 593-94 (2014).

8   Fed. Trade Comm'n, Self-Regulation and Privacy Online: A Report to Congress 12–14 (1999).

9   15 U.S.C. § 45(a)(1)-(2).

or clicking agree. Or they could go somewhere else, read that website's privacy policy, and consent to the data use practices of another platform.

This regime is largely based on a set of Fair Information Practice Principles (FIPPs) that themselves developed out of a 1973 report from the federal Department of Housing, Education, and Welfare (HEW).[10] The HEW Report recommended that users be informed of data use practices, have the opportunity to correct their data, and consent to any secondary uses of their information, among other things. Several years later, the Organization for Economic Co-operation and Development issued similar guidelines, requiring, for example, that data gatherers disclose the purpose and scope of data collection, any security protocols, and all user rights.[11] By 2000, the FTC identified "notice" as the most important FIPP, and notice-and-consent then became the dominant approach to consumer privacy.[12]

The FTC put notice requirements at the center of first wave of privacy law by suing companies that broke promises in their privacy policies. In *In re Eli Lilly & Co.*, for instance, the FTC alleged that the company violated its privacy policy when it sent out an email to nearly 700 people that disclosed personal information from customers who used the website Prozac.com. The company's privacy policy had promised "security measures" that would protect consumers' confidential information.[13] Since no such security measures had been in place, the company had broken its promise. *In re Toysmart.com* concerned another broken promise. During bankruptcy, Toysmart wanted to auction off a trove of customer data to

---

[10]   U.S. Dep't of Health, Educ., & Welfare, Records, Computers, and the Rights of Citizens: Report of the Secretary's Advisory Committee on Automated Personal Data Systems 41-42 (1973).

[11]   Organization for Economic Cooperation and Development (OECD), OECD Guidelines on the Protection of Privacy and Transborder Flows of Personal Data, at Part II (2001), https://www.oecd-ilibrary.org/docserver/9789264196391-en.pdf?expires=1685800025&id=id&accname=guest&checksum=B7B0099D4F8431AFE09C12721B924B6C.

[12]   FTC, Prepared Statement of the Federal Trade Commission on "Privacy Online: Fair Information Practices in the Electronic Marketplace", Before the Senate Committee on Commerce, Science, and Transportation § III(1) (May 25, 2000), https://www.ftc.gov/sites/default/files/documents/public_statements/prepared-statement-federal-trade-commission-privacy-online/testimonyprivacy.pdf.

[13]   *In re* Eli Lilly & Co., 133 F.T.C. 763, 765-67 (2002) (complaint).

pay its creditors even though the company had promised never to do so. The FTC sued Toysmart in federal court to prevent the sale, arguing that it violated the express terms of the Toysmart privacy policy and would constitute user deception if it went through.[14] The FTC has also moved against companies that have promised, yet failed, to collect only certain types of data,[15] to put in place adequate security safeguards,[16] and to maintain user anonymity,[17] to name just a few examples. Broken promise litigation, which, by its very nature, depends entirely on the particular disclosures in privacy policies, remains a significant share of the FTC's overall privacy enforcement actions.[18]

When the FTC eventually settled with these and other companies, its consent decrees further entrenched notice-and-consent as the core of first wave privacy law by requiring companies to include specific content in privacy policies. In its first privacy enforcement action, the FTC alleged that GeoCities sold its customers' personal information in express violation of its privacy policy.[19] As part of a settlement, the FTC ordered the company to disclose a what-when-how of data use: what information it collected, why it did so, to whom the information would be sold, and how customers could access their information and opt out.[20]

In *In re Frostwire, LLC*, for instance, the FTC alleged that the company, which developed peer-to-peer files-haring software, misled customers

---

[14] First Amended Complaint for Permanent Injunction and Other Equitable Relief, FTC v. Toysmart.com, LLC, No. 00-11341-RGS, at ¶ 11, 16-18 (D. Mass. July 21, 2000), http://www.ftc.gov/sites/default/files/documents/cases/toysmartcomplaint.htm.

[15] *E.g., In re* Microsoft Corp., 134 F.T.C. 709, 715 (2002) (complaint).

[16] *E.g.*, Complaint for Permanent Injunction and Other Equitable Relief ¶ 43, FTC v. Rennert, No. CV-S-00-0861-JBR (D. Nev. July 12, 2000), http://www.ftc.gov/sites/default/files/documents/cases/2000/07/ftc.gov-iogcomp.htm.

[17] Complaint, *In re* Compete, Inc., FTC File No. 102 3155, No. C-4384 ¶ 23 (F.T.C. Feb. 20, 2013), http://www.ftc.gov/sites/default/files/documents/cases/2013/02/130222competecmpt.pdf.

[18] Chris Jay Hoofnagle, Fed. Trade Comm'n Privacy Law and Policy 159-66 (2016); Solove & Hartzog, *supra* note 7, at 628-38.

[19] Complaint ¶¶ 13-14, *In re* GeoCities, F.T.C. File No. 982 3015, No. C-3850 (Aug. 13, 1998), https://www.ftc.gov/sites/default/files/documents/cases/1998/08/geo-cmpl.htm.

[20] Decision and Order, *In re* GeoCities, F.T.C. File No. 982 3015, No. C-3850 (Feb. 12, 1999), https://www.ftc.gov/sites/default/files/documents/cases/1999/02/9823015.do_.htm.

into thinking that certain files would not be publicly accessible on the peer-to-peer network. Frostwire also failed to adequately disclose how the software actually worked.[21] In *In re Sony BMG Music Entertainment*, the FTC alleged that Sony failed to inform customers that the software it installed on certain CDs would transmit music listening data back to Sony.[22] The FTC settled both cases. In each settlement, the FTC ordered Frostwire and Sony, respectively, to make specific what-when-how disclosures to its customers.

Almost all FTC enforcement actions settle.[23] Throughout the first wave of privacy law, these actions settled with some common recurring requirements, including notifying customers of a company's wrongdoing, making changes or additions to privacy policies, and informing users about those changes.[24] But for the most part, all of these early consent decrees focused on fixing, improving, and enhancing notice. They all stayed within the notice-and-consent framework and still allowed companies to make (or not make) their own promises about data use. The first wave put the onus of privacy navigation on the user, making the agreement between users and data collectors on the terms of a privacy policy the locus of the law's concern.[25]

Several federal and state laws also started requiring notices in certain contexts.[26] In the U.S., there are dozens of sector-specific federal and countless state laws that purport to protect information privacy. For example, the Health Information Portability and Accountability Act (HIPAA), which helps protect the privacy of medical information,[27] and

---

21   Complaint for Permanent Injunction and Other Equitable Relief at 19, FTC v. Frostwire, LLC, No. 1:11-cv-23643 (S.D. Fla. Oct. 12, 2011), http://www .ftc.gov/sites/default/files/documents/cases/2011/10/111011frostwirecmpt .pdf.

22   Complaint at 4, *In re* Sony BMG Music Entm't, F.T.C. File No. 062 3019, No. C-4195 (June 29, 2007), http://www.ftc.gov/sites/default/files/documents/ cases/2007/01/070130cmp0623019.pdf.

23   Solove and Hartzog, *supra* note 7, at 610–11.

24   *Id.* at 614–19.

25   Daniel J. Solove, *Introduction: Privacy Self-Management and the Consent Dilemma*, 126 Harv. L. Rev. 1880, 1899 (2013).

26   Solove and Hartzog, *supra* note 7, at 592.

27   Health Insurance Portability and Accountability Act of 1996, Pub. L. No. 104-191, 100 Stat. 2548 (1996) (codified as amended at 42 U.S.C. §§ 1320d(1)-(9)); 45 C.F.R. 164.528 (2016).

the Gramm-Leach-Bliley Act, which gives individuals notice and some control over information held by certain financial institutions,[28] require covered entities to provide notice of data use practices. State laws follow suit. California's Online Privacy Protection Act (CalOPPA) required commercial websites and other online service operators that collect information about California residents to, among other things, post a data use policy.[29] Like the policies envisioned by Gramm-Leach-Bliley and HIPAA, CalOPPA-compliant policies must contain specific disclosures: what information is collected, with whom it may be shared, how the data will be used, and how individuals will be notified about policy changes. These are all first wave laws: They focused almost exclusively on notice and consent.

In this regime, privacy law was primarily a self-regulatory affair, with industry making its own data use policies and individuals navigating their privacy preferences platform by platform.[30] That is why Daniel Solove, one of the academy's leading privacy scholars, called it "privacy self-management".[31] The first wave required individuals to read lengthy privacy policies, take in all of that information, and then either use the website or go somewhere else (assuming there was another option).

2.3   Justifications for the notice-and-consent regime

There are four primary justifications for this approach, such that it was, to privacy law. I present these justifications not because they are perfect or because I agree with them (they are not and I do not). I present them to situate notice-and-consent in larger conversations in law, politics, technology, and society and, hopefully, to present the strongest case possible for a position I will critique in the next chapter.

---

[28]   Gramm-Leach-Bliley Act (GLBA), Financial Services Modernization Act of 1999, Pub. L. 106-102, 113 Stat. 1338 (1999) (codified as amended at 15 U.S.C. §§ 6801-6809).

[29]   Cal. Bus. & Prof. Code §§ 22575–22579.

[30]   Woodrow Hartzog & Daniel J. Solove, *The Scope and Potential of FTC Data Protection*, 83 GEO. WASH. L. REV. 2230, 2235 (2015).

[31]   Solove, *supra* note 25, at 1881.

The first justification is that notice-and-consent and privacy self-management generally enhance autonomy, liberty, and freedom. As one leading scholar noted, "[p]roviding people with notice, access, and the ability to control their data is key to facilitating some autonomy in a world where decisions are increasingly being made about them with the use of personal data."[32] What is more, different people have different privacy preferences. Allowing individuals to make their own choices not only respects their dignity as autonomous human beings, but also facilitates a heterogeneous approach to privacy befitting a heterogeneous, diverse population.

But although giving people the chance to evaluate data use practices and choose whether or not to use that website seems to enhance autonomy, there couldn't really be heterogenous approaches to privacy under notice-and-consent when most companies just collect everything. Therefore, notice-and-consent needed a second justification—namely, people don't really care that much about privacy anyway. This justification relies on the so-called "privacy paradox"—people respond to surveys saying they want more privacy but behave in ways that suggest the opposite—to argue that their customers don't really want privacy.[33] If consumers did really want more privacy, the argument goes, they wouldn't be sharing and clicking and disclosing so much information. It's easy to fib on a survey—social scientists call it a social desirability bias—but consumers' actions speak louder than words. Best to give them the option to allow data collection under notice-and-consent in order to reap the benefits. Do as I do, not as I say.

The third justification for the first wave is a legal one. That is, making decisions after being informed about possible risks and benefits, and then being responsible for those decisions, has a long history in U.S. law. Informed consent and its underlying logics of autonomy are prominent in the laws and rules governing the doctor-patient relationship and medical privacy.[34] In the 1914 case *Schloendorf v. Society of New York*

---

32   *Id.* at 1899.
33   Patricia A. Norberg et al., *The Privacy Paradox: Personal Information Disclosure Intentions Versus Behavior*, 41 J. CONSUMER AFF. 100 (2007).
34   E.g., Joan H. Krause, *Reconceptualizing Informed Consent in an Era of Health Care Cost Containment*, 85 IOWA L. REV. 261, 267-78 (1999); Lawrence O. Gostin and James G. Hodge, Jr., *Personal Privacy and Common Goods: A Framework for Balancing Under the National Health*

Hospital,[35] Judge Benjamin Cardozo, sitting on the New York Court of Appeals, stated that "[e]very human being of adult years and sound mind has a right to determine what should be done with his own body."[36] The case was brought by a patient who claimed she was operated on without her consent, and Judge Cardozo affirmed her claim with a strong vision of informed consent as an essential aspect of autonomy.

Schloendorf's principle was affirmed repeatedly by the time *Salgo v. Leland Stanford Jr. University Board of Trustees* was decided in 1957.[37] In that case, an appeals court in California officially recognized a tort action for a doctor's failure to inform a patient about a procedure's known risks prior to obtaining consent for that procedure.[38] HIPAA is also an informed consent law; it enables sharing of medical information among certain medical professionals and health care organizations only after a patient affirms that they have read the risks of such sharing and agreed.[39] As these examples indicate, informed consent is a form of individual empowerment, giving us control over what happens to our bodies, our health, and our future. Notice-and-consent, the argument goes, merely extends that same idea to the digital world of websites, data, and technology.

The fourth justification for the first wave of notice-and-consent is probably the most honest and most frequently invoked by industry and their policymaker allies. That is, notice-and-consent offers limited regulation on purpose; anything more would stifle innovation. Innovation, industry says, is always a normative good. Innovation means new products, new opportunities for connection, new apps that automate and speed up old services, new consumer welfare, and new efficiencies. If we want a world where entrepreneurs are building the next exciting new technology, then law just has to get out of the way. Ajit Pai, former Chairman of the Federal Communications Commission and a former lawyer for Verizon,

---

Information Privacy Rule, 86 Minn. L. Rev. 1439, 1466-69 (2002); Richard C. Turkington, *Confidentiality Policy for HIV-Related Information: An Analytical Framework for Sorting Out Hard and Easy Cases*, 34 Vill. L. Rev. 871, 891-93 (1989).

35   105 N.E. 92 (N.Y. 1914).
36   *Id.* at 93.
37   317 P.2d 170 (Cal. Dist. Ct. App. 1957).
38   *Id.* at 181.
39   Uses and Disclosures Requiring an Opportunity for the Individual to Agree or to Object, 45 C.F.R. §§ 164.510–164.522.

has stated that telecommunications over the Internet is the "greatest free-market success story in history." Best we leave it that way, he said, calling for a "light-touch regulatory framework."[40] Other industry representatives have testified before Congress to argue that privacy law will stifle progress, make it difficult for companies to comply with the law, and place a particular burden on small business that lack the resources of their larger competitors. For example, the Interactive Advertising Bureau, an industry trade group, told the Senate Commerce Committee that privacy regulation will "impose significant burdens on consumers ... [and] also fail to recognize the ways in which digital advertising subsidizes the plentiful, varied, and rich digital content and services consumers use."[41] The Advertising Bureau's preferred legal response was more transparency, better notice, and more choice.

2.4   Meaning of privacy in the first wave

During this first wave, more restrictive privacy laws were attacked as "break[ing] the internet" and undermining a growing market of e-commerce and social media.[42] The idea that government would restrict itself to minimally enforcing other people's promises and letting companies make those promises however they want was not only wholly appropriate but also ideal. The best way, the first wave argued, to encourage innovation on the Internet was to have government get out of the way. Therefore, the first wave arguably reflected a "hands off," or classically liberal, approach to law and the information economy.[43]

---

40   Ajit Pai, The Future of Internet Freedom, https://transition.fcc.gov/Daily _Releases/Daily_Business/2017/db0427/DOC-344590A1.pdf.
41   U.S. Senate, Committee on Commerce, Science, and Transportation. *Policy Principles for a Federal Data Privacy Framework in the United States.* 116th Cong. 1st sess. (2019) (written testimony of Randall Rothenberg, CEO of the Interactive Advertising Bureau).
42   Danielle Keats Citron and Benjamin Wittes, *The Internet Will Not Break: Denying Bad Samaritans § 230 Immunity,* 86 FORDHAM L. REV. 401, 401 (2017).
43   Classical liberalism "sought to define an area of social life standing outside of . . . political governance and not appropriate for political decision." David Singh Grewal and Jedediah Purdy, *Introduction: Law and Neoliberalism,* 77 L. & CONTEMP. PROBS. 1, 10 (2014).

Hand in hand with that *laissez faire* approach to the relationship between government and the economy came a similar hands-off understanding of privacy. If first wave privacy law focused almost exclusively on giving individuals notice of data use practices and the opportunity to consent to that data extraction, then its underlying conception of privacy must be one of autonomy and choice. Privacy-as-choice or privacy-as-autonomy (I will use privacy-as-choice for short) refers to thinking about privacy as the right to determine for oneself what, when, and to whom to disclose information about ourselves.[44] In other words, privacy is a manifestation of the choosing self, exercising their autonomy to pursue the good life however they want. That could mean giving up their data for access to digital services, targeted advertisements, and the ease of skipping the security line at the airport. It could also mean a preference for privacy-preserving technologies like the Firefox web browser or the encrypted Signal mobile app. Or, of course, it could mean something in between. The point is: it doesn't matter. That's what autonomy is principally about.

This idea has a long scholarly tradition. Jean Cohen argues that privacy is the right "to choose whether, when, and with whom" to share intimate information.[45] Charles Fried suggests that different groups of friends exist because we actively choose to share more with intimate friends and less with acquaintances.[46] This free choice gives us the right to control public knowledge of our personal selves. Privacy, then, "is the claim of individuals, groups, or institutions to determine for themselves when, how, and to what extent information about them is communicated to others."[47] For the philosopher Steve Matthews, exercising privacy is making the choice to "manage" the boundary between ourselves and others.[48] The common denominator in all these descriptions is free choice, both of which are central an ideal of rights that is at the foundation of liberalism.[49]

---

[44]   Ari Ezra Waldman, Privacy As Trust 29-33 (2019); Daniel J. Solove, Understanding Privacy 24-29 (2008).

[45]   Jean L. Cohen, *The Necessity of Privacy*, 68 Soc. Res. 318, 319 (2001).

[46]   Charles Fried, *Privacy*, 77 Yale L.J. 475, 484 (1968).

[47]   Alan F. Westin, Privacy and Freedom 7 (1967).

[48]   Steve Matthews, *Anonymity and the Social Self*, 47 Am. Phil. Q. 351, 351 (2010).

[49]   *See, e.g.*, John Locke, Second Treatise of Government § 123, at 66 (C.B. Macpherson ed. 1980) (1690); Immanuel Kant, Groundwork of the Metaphysic of Morals 71-72 (H.J. Paton trans. 1964) (1785); John Rawls, A Theory of Justice (1971).

Privacy-as-choice has certain benefits. A sense of autonomy is powerful and empowering, and it is deeply rooted—for better and for worse—in popular legal and political consciousness in the U.S. This conception of privacy also allows for variability in privacy preferences where a one-size-fits-all approach might strike some as paternalistic or coercive. After all, it is a fact that lots of people may have very different privacy preferences; a single person might have different privacy preferences in different contexts. Better let each of us choose for ourselves how much privacy we want in any given circumstance. As we will see in the next chapter, however, the choosing self and the first wave of privacy law it undergirds are utter disempowering, denying us the very autonomy privacy-as-choice promises.

3 The illusions of the first wave

At least on the surface, notice-and-consent is about autonomy, empowerment, and individual choice. If those who collected and used our data would just explain themselves clearly, we could make informed decisions about whether or not we wanted to give up our data and have it used and shared in the information economy. After all, not everyone has the same privacy preferences. I might not want Facebook tracking my every move, but some might want Google to know enough about them to provide expertly tailored search results. Notice-and-consent, then, is privacy self-governance.

As Daniel Solove has written, privacy self-governance "involves the various decisions people must make about their privacy and the tasks people are given the choice to do regarding their privacy, such as reading privacy policies, opting out, changing privacy settings, and so on."[1] Can most of us actually do that, though? We might be able to make decisions about our lives when given time, details, and education, but can we make those choices at scale, meaning every time we open a mobile app or a website? We cannot. Privacy law's first wave collapsed long ago. It's four foundational assumptions—none of which stand up to scrutiny—are as follows: (1) that we can adequately process the information in privacy policies, (2) that our decision-making based on that information is perfectly rational (or at least rational-ish), (3) that when we give consent—click "Agree" or shift a toggle—we are actually making a real choice, and

---

[1] Daniel J. Solove, *The Myth of the Privacy Paradox*, 89 Geo. Wash. L. Rev. 1, 5 (2021).

(4) that consent is actually an empowering thing online. Let's discuss each in turn.[2]

3.1 The illusion of comprehension at scale

Privacy notices are difficult to parse, written in language even experts cannot always understand, and sit in the annoying space between users and access to the content they want. Notices are supposed to give us the information we need to make informed decisions.[3] But we can't access that information in any effective way. Aleecia McDonald and Lorrie Faith Cranor found that it would take us nearly 244 hours per year to read all the privacy policies of the websites we visit.[4] Few people are doing that. Maybe you'll read them if you're a student an information privacy class, a privacy professional or lawyer for a technology company, or a staff attorney at the FTC. I'm sure some others read them, too. But for the most part, the information inside privacy privacies is simply inaccessible. As a result, consumers enter into transactions with technology platforms without any meaningful tools to make adequate and informed decision-making.

Notice may be effective in discrete decision-making—when we have to make one decision about one choice. But notice-and-consent doesn't scale.[5] A physician tells us the medical risks associated with one pro-

---

2   Much of this chapter is adapted, with permission, from ARI EZRA WALDMAN, INDUSTRY UNBOUND: THE INSIDE STORY OF PRIVACY, DATA, AND CORPORATE POWER 52-57 (2021).

3   George R. Milne and Mary J. Culnan, Strategies for Reducing Online Privacy Risks: Why Consumers Read (or Don't Read) Online Privacy Policies, 18 J. INTERACTIVE MARKETING 15 (2004); Lorrie F. Cranor, Necessary but Not Sufficient: Standardized Mechanisms for Privacy Notice and Choice, 10 J. TELECOM. & HIGH TECH. L. 273, 274 (2012); Joel R. Reidenberg, Disagreeable Privacy Policies: Mismatches Between Meaning and Users' Understanding, 30 BERKELEY TECH. L.J. 39 (2014).

4   Aleecia M. McDonald and Lorrie F. Cranor, The Cost of Reading Privacy Policies, 4 I/S: J. L. & POL'Y INFO. SOC'Y 543, 563 (2008).

5   Daniel J. Solove, Introduction: Privacy Self-Management and the Consent Dilemma, 126 HARV. L. REV. 1880 (2013); Neil Richards and Woodrow Hartzog, The Pathologies of Digital Consent, 96 WASH. U. L. REV. 1461 (2019).

cedure and a financial adviser tells us the benefits and risks of certain investments. They can sit in front of us, give us the space to ask questions, discuss alternatives, and engage in a holistic approach to their jobs and their advice. It should come as no surprise, then, as we learned in Chapter 1, that the whole idea of informed consent in U.S. law solidified in the healthcare context.

But applying that same idea to the information economy today asks us to know how every single mobile app, website, WiFi-enabled gadget, and streaming platform, among so many other technologies, collects, shares, and uses our data. True informed consent also demands that we understand all of the known consequences of that data collection and use. Our data could be used to target us for advertisements and sales, but it could also be integrated into machine learning tools that aim to predict what we want and enable companies to create digital environments that trigger or goad us into spending money on what they want us to spend money on.

And if it weren't difficult enough to read, analyze, and integrate the notices of, say, the 50 websites we visit in a day, there is another problem besides decision fatigue and our inability to comprehend the myriad downstream, manipulative consequences of data collection at scale. There are hundreds of websites we never see that track us, monitor our browsing behavior, and share our information with others. Those platforms may have posted privacy policies somewhere, but we can't look for something we don't know is there. It should come as no surprise, then, that we have no idea what we're doing when companies ask us to consent to something. Studies by Joe Turow, Nora Draper, and others demonstrate that only 30 percent of nonexpert respondents correctly understand the privacy (or lack thereof) associated with their online transactions. Nearly two-thirds of people do not realize that a supermarket is allowed to sell information about purchasing habits to other companies. And, remarkably, almost 75 percent of people falsely believe that when "a website has a privacy policy, it means the site will not share [their] ... information with other websites and companies."[6]

---

[6]   Joseph Turow et al., The Tradeoff Fallacy: How Marketers Are Misrepresenting American Consumers and Opening Them Up to Exploitation. A Report from the Annenberg Public Policy Center of the University of Pennsylvania, https://repository.upenn.edu/cgi/viewcontent .cgi?article=1554&hx0026;context=asc_papers; Joseph Turow et al., Open

Internet users have to navigate platform settings to match their privacy preferences but feel resigned to failure because of a perception that privacy violations are unavoidable. Scholars have found that users feel powerless and helpless.[7] This leads to what Draper and Turow have called "digital resignation": We give up when we see how hard it is to protect our privacy or navigate opt-outs, consents, and cookie requests online.[8] We don't just stop trying to protect our privacy; we also give up the expectation that it's even possible. Along with Turow, Draper, and Yphtach Lelkes, all scholars of communication studies, I was a co-author on a 2023 report issued by the Annenberg Center for Communication at the University of Pennsylvania entitled, *Americans Can't Consent to Companies' Use of Their Data*.[9] The report describes the result of a study that surveyed 2,014 U.S. adults and asked them to answer a series of true/false questions about data collection in surveillance economy. Most people got most of the answers wrong. For instance, 75 percent of respondents think the federal government "regulates the types of digital information companies collect about individuals." It does not. Almost as many people said they did not have "the time to keep up with the ways to control the information that companies" had about them. Lack of comprehension plus fatigue is the perfect recipe for data extraction.

Along similar lines, Professor Solove notes that:

> [m]anaging one's privacy is a vast, complex, and never-ending project ... . The best people can do is manage their privacy haphazardly. People can't learn

---

to Exploitation: America's Shoppers Online and Offline. A Report from the Annenberg Public Policy Center of the University of Pennsylvania (2005), https://repository.upenn.edu/cgi/viewcontent.cgi?article=1035&context= asc_papers.

7   Alice Marwick and Eszter Hargittai, Nothing to Hide, Nothing to Lose? Incentives and Disincentives to Sharing Information With Institutions Online, 22 INFO. COMM. & SOC'Y 1697 (2018); Eszter Hargittai and Alice Marwick, What Can I Really Do? Explaining the Privacy Paradox with Online Apathy 10 INT'L J. COMM. 3737 (2016).

8   Nora Draper and Joseph Turow, *The Corporate Cultivation of Digital Resignation*, 21 NEW MEDIA & SOC'Y 1824 (2019).

9   Joseph Turow et al., *Americans Can't Consent to Companies' Use of Their Data*, Annenberg School of Communications, University of Pennsylvania (Feb. 2023), https://www.asc.upenn.edu/sites/default/files/ 2023-02/Americans_Can%27t_Consent.pdf; Natasha Singer, *Americans Flunked this Test on Online Privacy*, N.Y. TIMES (Feb. 7, 2023), https://www .nytimes.com/2023/02/07/technology/online-privacy-tracking-report.html.

enough about privacy risks to make informed decisions about their privacy. People will never gain sufficient knowledge of the ways in which personal data will be combined, aggregated, and analyzed over the years by thousands of organizations.[10]

No one can sufficiently and adequately estimate the risk of future harm, especially when those harms are not disclosed and the current practices that could lead to those harms are buried in legalese, small font size, and overlong policies. Most people do not have the time or energy or cognitive ability to even translate what's written in a privacy policy to any kind of harm.

Privacy self-governance turns us into nihilists. Notice-and-consent isn't liberational and autonomy-enhancing. It transforms us into passive users, accepting the power that corporations have over us because there doesn't seem to be anything we can do about it. Informed consent, therefore, is illusory in the digital and online contexts at scale.

3.2   The illusion of rationality

Notice-and-consent also relies on the assumption that we make perfectly rational decisions. That is, the notion that individuals' true privacy preferences will be expressed by choices made after reading a detailed notice of data use practices implies that we take in that information, balance the pros and cons, and opt for the option that best fits our needs. Although an important piece of privacy scholarship to date, perfect rationality is a myth.

Rationality used to be a foundational principle in the privacy literature. Alan Westin, one of the earliest leading privacy scholars, identifies three categories of consumers: privacy "fundamentalists", "unconcerned", and "pragmatists". Fundamentalists cared a lot about privacy, the unconcerned cared little, and the pragmatists mediated between them by making decisions case-by-case.[11] Richard Posner brought an economic

---

[10]   Solove, *Myth*, *supra* note 1, at 5.

[11]   U.S. House of Representatives, Subcommittee on Commerce, Trade, and Consumer Protection of the House Committee on Energy and Commerce, Opinion Surveys: What Consumers Have to Say About Information Privacy.

analysis to disclosure, arguing that individuals tend to weigh the pros and cons prior to disclosure.[12] Rationality remains a bedrock assumption among policymakers who argue that the purpose of more detailed, more conspicuous, and more accurate notices is to help people make better choices. For example, in its report entitled, *Protecting Consumer Privacy in an Era of Rapid Change*, the FTC stated that "privacy statements should contain some standardized elements, such as format and terminology, to allow consumers to compare the privacy practices of different companies."[13] The whole idea of comparing privacy practices, especially based on a standardized "nutrition label" for privacy, suggests that the FTC envisions us weighing pros and cons. Companies also insist that they will be more transparent specifically so we can engage more deeply and discern what we want to see from what may be misleading us.[14] And during Facebook CEO Mark Zuckerberg's testimony before the U.S. Senate in 2018, Republican Senator Chuck Grassley of Iowa stated that "consumers must have the transparency necessary to make an informed decision about whether to share their data and how it can be used" and explicitly linked transparency, understanding, and decision-making.[15]

And yet, it is hard to argue we are acting rationally when we click "Agree". Even if we read privacy policies, the choices we make are not siloed from the context in which we make them. Psychologists Daniel Kahneman and Amos Tversky demonstrate that mental shortcuts and cognitive biases dominate our decision-making processes.[16] Instead of rationally weighing

---

107th Cong., 1st sess. H. Hearing Record (2000) (prepared statement of Alan F. Westin).

12   Richard Posner, *The Right of Privacy*, 12 GA. L. REV. 393 (1978).

13   Fed. Trade Comm'n, Protecting Consumer Privacy in an Era of Rapid Change 62 (2015).

14   Mark Zuckerberg, When Someone Buys Political Ads on TV or Other Media, They're Required by Law to Disclose Who Paid for Them. Now We're Bringing Facebook to an Even Higher Standard of Transparency, FACEBOOK (October 27, 2017), https://www.facebook.com/zuck/posts/10104133053040371.

15   U.S. Senate, Committee on Commerce, Science, and Transportation, *Facebook, Social Media Privacy, and the Use and Abuse of Data.* 115th Cong., 2d sess. S. Hearing Record (2018) (oral statement of Senator Grassley).

16   DANIEL KAHNEMAN, THINKING, FAST AND SLOW (2011); Daniel Kahneman and Amos Tversky, *Judgments of and By Representativeness, in* JUDGMENT UNDER UNCERTAINTY: HEURISTICS AND BIASES 84-98 (Daniel Kahneman,

risks and benefits when making a decision—almost any decision, not just about our data and privacy online—we are more likely to use heuristics and first impressions, even when those shortcuts lead us astray. So, for example, instead of judging a book by its content, we judge it by its cover, recommendations from friends, marketing materials, and whether we liked a book written by the same author before, among other short cuts.

Researchers have found that we often rely on comparative judgments when making disclosure decisions: if we perceive that others are willing to disclose, we are more likely to disclose.[17] The psychologist and Harvard Business School Professor Leslie K. John has also found that individuals online are more willing to disclose bad behavior on websites that have an unprofessional aesthetic.[18] Apparently, users perceive those websites as more informal and less series, like chatting with a friend. Other researchers have found that our subjective assessment of privacy's importance is not the primary mover of our willingness to disclose personal information.[19] As Will Oremus has noted, "study after study has found that people's valuations of data privacy are driven less by rational assessments of the risks they face than by factors like the wording of the questions they're asked, the information they're given beforehand, and the range of choices they're presented."[20]

Our decision-making is also influenced by design. Richard Thaler and Cass Sunstein have shown in a series of works how "choice architecture," or the designed contexts in which people make decisions, can "alter people's behavior in a predictable way without forbidding any options," like how grouping expensive cereals at eye-level and relegating the cheaper

---

Paul Slovic and Amos Tversky eds. 2011); Daniel Kahneman and Amos Tversky, *Judgment Under Uncertainty: Heuristics and Biases*, 185 SCIENCE 1124 (1974).

[17]   Alessandro Acquisiti et al., *The Impact of Relative Standards on the Propensity to Disclose*, 49 J. MARKETING RES. 160 (2012).

[18]   Leslie K. John et al., *Strangers on a Plane: Context-Dependent Willingness to Divulge Sensitive Information*, 37 J. CONSUMER RES. 858 (2011).

[19]   Ari Ezra Waldman and James A. Mourey, *Past the Privacy Paradox: The Important of Privacy Changes as a Function of Control and Complexity*, 5 J. ASSOC. CONSUMER RES. 162 (2020).

[20]   Will Oremus, *How Much Is Your Privacy Really Worth? No One Knows. And It Might be Time to Stop Asking*, MEDIUM (Sept. 17, 2019), https://onezero .medium.com/how-much-is-your-privacy-really-worth-421796dd9220.

ones below encourages a more expensive purchase.[21] Reflecting on their study of digital games, Mary Flanigan and Helen Nissenbaum, a technologist and social theorist of technology, respectively, long ago recognized that technology designers can control what happens in their constructed spaces; their "semantic architecture" tells the story designers want to tell, much in the same way designers of spaces and objects direct and guide their use.[22] And the privacy scholar Woodrow Hartzog has demonstrated how almost everything we do online is manipulated by the design—from aesthetics to code—of built digital environments.[23]

It is, therefore, difficult to see how notice-and-consent is supposed to function as a system of informed consent. If a company can design its platform to goad us into disclosure, if it can design its privacy policy to make us ignore or skip over it, if it can nudge us with design tricks that cue us to make whatever decision the company wants rather than what we want, then notice-and-consent is either negligent or willfully blind to its facilitation of manipulation. Sharing is contingent on both our mental capacity and constraints placed on us by designers. By making the process of navigating our privacy choices easier or harder, platform designers can tinker with us. Therefore, our clicks are not manifestations of our autonomous decisions about anything. Rather, they reflect manipulated responses to platform design. As the media scholar Siva Vaidhyanathan has stated, people's privacy choices online "mean very little" because "the design of the system rigs it in favor of the interests of the company and against the interests of users."[24]

Let's assume just for the moment that there remain pieces of rationality in that puzzle of manipulation. Surely some of us can pierce the power of nudges and coercive design to make choices that reflect our preferences. In fact, industry and its representatives often like to fall back on personal anecdotes of their or their friends' ability to decide for themselves what marketing emails they want. They don't seem to realize that anecdotes

---

21   RICHARD H. THALER AND CASS R. SUNSTEIN, NUDGE: IMPROVING DECISIONS ABOUT HEALTH, WEALTH, AND HAPPINESS (2008).
22   MARY FLANIGAN AND HELEN NISSENBAUM, VALUES AT PLAY IN DIGITAL GAMES 33 (2016); DONALD NORMAN, THE DESIGN OF EVERYDAY THINGS (1988).
23   WOODROW HARTZOG, PRIVACY'S BLUEPRINT (2019).
24   SIVA VAIDHYANATHAN, THE GOOGLIZATION OF EVERYTHING (AND WHY WE SHOULD WORRY) 83 (2011).

aren't evidence and, for the most part, the evidence is there that the steps we have to take in order to navigate privacy choices online are simply burdensome. We go website by website, app by app, sometimes making many choices per platform. We are responsible for reading privacy policies. We are tasked with finding alternative platforms—if they even exist—when we object to data collection practices. We have to navigate a platform's opt-out process. And we have to do this within an environment designed to extract our information. Indeed, the onus of protecting our privacy is almost entirely on our shoulders. That burden is too heavy to bear.

3.3   The illusion of real choice

Notice-and-consent wants us to believe that consent is the same thing as choice. As we have seen, consent can be a source of power. In other areas of law, we consent to medical procedures only after full disclosure of risks and benefits. The law of sexual assault gives us the power to consent to intimate touching and sexual encounters, and gives us important tools to protect that power.[25] But in those and in many other areas, our consent comes in the context of choice. We (usually) have the choice not to have this or that medical procedure; we (usually) have the choice to not engage sexually with someone else. We even (usually) have the choice to engage sexually with lots of other people; we can even get that surgery from another doctor at a different hospital. However, in the information economy, our consent to data collection comes without real alternatives.

In the most basic sense, there is little to no choice in the information economy because lax antitrust enforcement has allowed just a handful of companies to dominate the market. In 2020, Google accounted for nearly 93 percent of the search engine market. It's next competitor, Microsoft's Bing, had 3.03 percent.[26] Facebook dominates the social media market

---

[25]   Brian Murray, Informed Consent: What Must a Physician Disclose to a Patient?, 14 AMA J. ETHICS 563 (2012); State in Interest of M.T.S., 609 A.2d 1266 (N.J. 1992); United States v. Riley, 183 F.3d 1155 (9th Cir. 1999); United States v. Johnson, 743 F.3d 196 (7th Cir. 2014).

[26]   Search Engine Market Share Worldwide, Jan 2022-Jan 2023, Statscounter Global Stats, https://gs.statcounter.com/search-engine-market-share.

because it owns WhatsApp and Instagram.[27] Of course, all that can change, but that kind of domination is hard to dislodge. Therefore, if we really wanted to use a different search engine, it would be difficult. We certainly could switch: DuckDuckGo is a notable alternative because it is privacy protective. But companies like Google and Facebook (and Apple and insert any number of other Big Tech companies) trap users by leveraging their size, market power, and interoperable code. There just aren't enough other options out there to make notice-and-consent a means of effectuating real choice.

There are also downstream uses of data that are simply unknowable to us at the time of consent. For example, did Facebook users consent to participate in the company's emotional manipulation studies in 2014, in which the company subjected its users to negatively or positively framed information in order to see its effects on engagement?[28] In one sense, yes, by agreeing to Facebook's broad data use policy in its terms of service that could be read to incorporate the entire future universe of data uses. But in the most proximate sense, of course not, because no one consented to be part of this particular study. Similarly, although Facebook users may consent to share their "likes" with Facebook, they cannot seriously be permitting Facebook to learn everything it does from that "like," especially since that generated information can be deeply personal. For example, Facebook could tell that "users who liked the 'Hello Kitty' brand tended to high on Openness and low on 'Conscientiousness,' 'Agreeableness,' and 'Emotional Stability.' They were also more likely to have Democratic political views and to be of African-American origin[] [and] predominantly Christian."[29] This is just one of myriad correlations Facebook can make from its trove of data about us. But someone's willingness to

---

[27] Most Popular Social Networks Worldwide as of January 2022, Ranked by Number of Active Users, Statista, https://www.statista.com/statistics/272014/global-social-networks-ranked-by-number-of-users/.

[28] Catherine Flick, Informed Consent and the Facebook Emotional Manipulation Study, 21 RESEARCH ETHICS 14 (2015); David Talbot, Facebook's Emotional Manipulation Study is Just the Latest Effort to Prod Users, MIT TECH REV. (July 1, 2014), https://www.technologyreview.com/2014/07/01/172175/facebooks-emotional-manipulation-study-is-just-the-latest-effort-to-prod-users/.

[29] Adam Kramer et al., *Experimental Evidence of Massive-Scale Emotional Contagion Through Social Networks*, 111 PROCEEDINGS OF THE NAT'L ACAD. SCI. 8788 (2014).

disclose that they enjoy Hello Kitty cannot imply a similar willingness to disclose emotional, political, and racial information. It is, in other words, impossible to say those who consent to data collection are making a real choice to accept all that comes with data collection.

Consent is also easy to manipulate and manufacture, making free and autonomous choice unlikely. Platforms can use dark patterns to make it seem like accepting cookies, geotracking, or surveillance is the only option. Dark patterns are "interface design choices that benefit an online service by coercing, steering, or deceiving users into making decisions that, if fully informed and capable of selecting alternatives, they might not make."[30] And they are common.[31] Designers use dark patterns to hide, deceive, and goad. They confuse by asking questions in ways most people cannot understand, they obfuscate by hiding interface elements that could help protect privacy, they require registration and associated disclosures in order to access functionality, and they hide malicious behavior in the abyss of fine print. Policymakers should not expect us to act rationally when they have left in place a business model that does everything it can to trigger us to act against our own interest.

What is more, designers can frame opting out of data collection as tantamount to lack of functionality. We see this throughout the digital ecosystem: The social practices of consent are "Accept" buttons that have no "Reject" buttons, "Click I AGREE to continue," consent by continued use, take-it-or-leave-it privacy terms, and manipulative consent interfaces. And if consent is easy to manufacture, then consent isn't our own. Nor does it serve our interests. Rather, it is the product of manipulation in service of someone else's (usually) contradictory goals.

---

[30]   Arunesh Mathur, Gunes Acar, Michael J. Friedman, Eli Lucherini, Jonathan Mayer, Marshini Chetty and Arvind Narayanan, *Dark Patterns at Scale: Findings from a Crawl of 11K Shopping Websites*, 3 PROC. ACM ON HUM.-COMPUT. INTERACTION 1, 2 (2019).

[31]   See *id.*

3.4   The weaponization of consent against individuals

On the misleading premise that individuals are capable of making their own informed choices about what they share and with whom they share it, industry weaponizes consent in ways that make it almost meaningless. Consent, therefore, is a tool of power, not resistance.

In 2019, for instance, while Facebook was trying to dismiss a lawsuit for the company's failure to stop Cambridge Analytica from unlawfully mining user data, the company's attorney told Judge Vince Chhabria that "[t]here is no privacy interest" in any information Facebook has.[32] Users "consent[ed]" to the terms of service and engaged in "an affirmative social act to publish," which "under centuries of common law, ... negated any reasonable expectation of privacy."[33] When the judge asked if it would be an invasion of privacy for Facebook to break a promise not to share an individual's information with third parties, Facebook's counsel claimed that "Facebook does not consider that to be actionable," citing user behavior and consents as evidence that users had given up control of their data.[34] In its briefing, the company went even further, arguing that because individuals "can control how" their content is shared, anything they then share is ripe for use by Facebook and third parties.[35]

In *Campbell v. St. John*,[36] a case about Facebook's practice of scanning users' private messages to collect data for behavioral advertising, Facebook argued that users lacked standing to challenge any Facebook data practice because they "consented to the uses of ... data."[37] In *Smith v. Facebook*,[38] the company made the same argument, noting that Facebook

---

[32]   *In re* Facebook, Inc. Consumer Privacy User Profile Litigation, No. 18-MD-02843, May 29, 2019 (transcript of proceedings at 7).

[33]   *Id.*

[34]   *Id.* at 15.

[35]   Reply in Support of Defendant Facebook, Inc. to Dismiss Plaintiffs' First Amended Consolidated Complaint, *In re* Facebook, Inc. Consumer Privacy User Profile Litigation, 402 F. Supp 767, 792 (N.D. Cal. 2019).

[36]   No. 17–16873, 4:13-cv-05996-PJH (9th Cir. 2020), https://epic.org/amicus/class-action/facebook-campbell/Campbell-v-Facebook-9th-Cir-Opinion.pdf.

[37]   *Id.* at 21 n. 9.

[38]   No. 17–16206 (9th Cir. 2017).

should be allowed to track users wherever they go on the Internet because users "are bound by their consent to those policies."[39] And in *In re Google, Inc. Cookie Placement Consumer Privacy Litigation*,[40] Google moved to dismiss all claims pertaining to the unauthorized use of cookie tracking and the unlawful interception of user data by arguing that "both Plaintiffs and the websites they communicated with provided their consent for Google ... when they sent a GET request ... so that they could browse websites containing Google ads."[41] In other words, Google claimed that the mere use of its search engine is tantamount to consent to all of Google's data use practices, putting the burden of any consequences on the individual user.

Similarly, in *Patel v. Facebook*,[42] which challenged the company's collection and use of biometric information, Facebook argued that no plaintiff could ever successfully bring a lawsuit against the company for use of any kind of information, let alone biometric data, because "plaintiffs knew exactly what data Facebook was collecting, for what purpose, and how to opt out of Tag Suggestions."[43] Facebook suggested that this immunity was so broad that it held up even if the company's notices were not sufficiently specific.[44] Facebook reasoned that since users consented to all data collection practices when they signed up for accounts, and since privacy law only requires choice, consent, and control, users who signed up but never opted out had given up their rights to their data.[45]

Facebook has even argued that its own privacy promises are meaningless because it had the power to define the rights of its customers. For example, in several ongoing lawsuits, Facebook has argued that its promise to remove cookies that identify a particular user's account was

---

[40]   No. 13–4300, 2014 WL 1413954 (3rd Cir. Apr. 7, 2014).
[41]   Answering Brief of Defendant-Appellee Google Inc., *In re* Google Inc. Cookie Placement Consumer Privacy Litigation, No. 13–4300, 2014 WL 1413954, at 36–37 (3rd Cir. Apr. 7, 2014).
[42]   932 F.3d 1264 (9th Cir. 2019).
[43]   Appellant's Brief at 33, Patel v. Facebook, 932 F.3d 1264 (9th Cir. 2019).
[44]   Facebook, Inc.'s Motion for Summary Judgment, *In re* Facebook Biometric Information Privacy Litigation, 185 F. Supp. 1115 (N.D. Cal. 2016).
[45]   *Id.*

not a "promise[] not to record the communication[]" and that promises of anonymity do not create expectations of privacy.[46] In the same case, Facebook argued that all user information available to Facebook— including every website users visit—is "voluntarily disclosed."[47] It is easy to see the company making similar arguments on the ground that individuals are freely capable of exercising their rights of access, deletion, correction, and opt out, holding users responsible for all data use practices that result.

3.5   Conclusion

In the end, then, operationalizing consent in the privacy space achieves the exact opposite of individual control and empowerment. As one leading privacy scholar put it, the information industry "take[s] refuge in consent" to absolve them of their data protection responsibilities because "[c]onsent legitimizes nearly every form of collection, use, or disclosure of personal data."[48] Like notice, consent doesn't scale. Woodrow Hartzog has argued that "[w]e can feel so overwhelmed by the thousands of requests for access, permission, and consent to use our data that we say yes just because we are so worn down."[49] That's not control; that's beating us down until we give up and sign away our rights like an innocent arrestee under intense interrogation. Our consent isn't free. Decades ago, Joel Reidenberg noted that notice-and-consent was being sold to us as "predicated on the philosophy that self-regulation will accomplish the most meaningful protection of privacy without intrusive government interference, and with the greatest flexibility for dynamically developing technologies."[50] Well, we were sold a lemon.

---

46   Defendant Facebook, Inc.'s Reply in Support of Motion to Dismiss Plaintiffs' Second Amendment Consolidated Complaint, *In re* Facebook, Inc. Internet Tracking Litigation, 263 F. Supp 836 at 11 (N.D. Cal. 2017).

47   Defendant Facebook, Inc.'s Motion to Dismiss Plaintiffs' Second Amended Consolidated Complaint, *In re* Facebook, Inc. Internet Tracking Litigation, 263 F. Supp 836 at 33 (N.D. Cal. 2017).

48   Solove, *Privacy Self-Management, supra* note 5, at 1880.

49   WOODROW HARTZOG, PRIVACY'S BLUEPRINT 208 (2018).

50   Joel R. Reidenberg, *Restoring Americans' Privacy in Electronic Commerce*, 14 BERKELEY TECH. L.J. 771, 774 (1999).

And first wave privacy law knowingly sold us that lemon. What is sold to us as notice-and-consent has been weaponized by industry to saddle us with the responsibility for whatever tech companies want to do with our data. What is sold as rationality is weaponized against regulation as evidence of consumer demand. What is sold as self-governance is weaponized against regulation and legal accountability, a tactic the law and information scholar Julie Cohen calls the "surveillance-innovation complex".[51] Notice-and-consent, then, is less a discourse about privacy than it is a discourse about corporate power and immunity from regulation.

---

[51]   Julie E. Cohen, Between Truth and Power: Legal Constructions of Informational Capitalism 89, 96-97, 102-104 (2019).

PART II

PRIVACY LAW'S SECOND WAVE

4 Rights and compliance

We are now in the middle of privacy law's second wave. Between 2018 and 2021, 11 proposals for comprehensive privacy legislation were introduced in Congress. During that same time, two ballot initiatives and 40 privacy bills were introduced in 28 states.[1] As of this writing, in early 2023, five states have comprehensive privacy laws on the books; 16 states have 34 privacy bills under active consideration.[2] These proposals come in the wake of the General Data Protection Regulation (GDPR) in the European Union and the California Consumer Privacy Act (CCPA), with more likely on the way. Remarkably, almost all of them look similar: They combine a series of individual rights with internal compliance structures. It's a legal regime that the legal scholar Margot Kaminski has called "binary governance".[3]

4.1   What are the rights?

In addition to first wave rights to notice-and-consent, second wave laws like the Utah Consumer Privacy Act add new individual rights, including rights to access all the personal information the company has about us, have a company delete the personal information it has already collected, and opt out of tracking or the sale or transfer of data to third parties.[4] Some proposals include rights against retaliation for exercising opt-out

---

[1]   For the full list of all of these bills, please see Ari Ezra Waldman, *The New Privacy Law*, 55 U.C. Davis L. Rev. 19, 21-22 (2021).

[2]   Int'l Assoc. of Privacy Professionals, US State Privacy Legislation Tracker, Comprehensive Consumer Privacy Bills 2023, https://iapp.org/resources/article/us-state-privacy-legislation-tracker/.

[3]   Margot E. Kaminski, *Binary Governance: Lessons from the GDPR's Approach to Algorithmic Accountability*, 92 S. Cal. L. Rev. 1529 (2019).

[4]   S.B. 227, Utah Consumer Privacy Act, § 13–61–201.

rights, rights to correct inaccurate or outdated data, rights to move data from one company to another, and rights to restrict processing of personal data. Several draft bills include opt-in rights for certain types of data collection and processing. The proposed New York Privacy Act would give citizens a right against purely algorithmic or automated decisions about their lives. And in addition to many of the rights above, the Privacy Bill of Rights would guarantee a right to data security. The Data Accountability and Transparency Act, or DATA, guarantees a right to object to data processing and human review of automated decision-making systems.[5]

Notably, some second wave privacy laws also build on the first wave's consent paradigm. Almost all state and federal proposals in the U.S. are opt-out regimes, which means that data collection and processing is presumed lawful unless individuals affirmatively withdraw their consent. Some laws go further, doubling down on the power of consent. For instance, two proposals in Arizona allow companies that obtain consent to sell customer data, avoid all restrictions on data processing, and make decisions about the consumer based on consent.[6] Two proposals introduced in the Illinois Senate would allow companies to skirt limits on processing sensitive data, even processing that posed a significant risk to privacy, if they obtain consent.[7] And Maine's privacy law, which took effect in 2020, lifts all restrictions on use, disclosure, sale, and third-party access to personal information if companies obtain consent.[8]

Guaranteeing these rights gives rise to two sets of social practices: individuals have to exercise their rights and companies have to develop processes to evaluate customer requests. To opt out of certain data processing, for example, individuals must click on a link and complete a form. Indeed, they have to take the initiative to exercise almost all second wave rights. Companies also have to build forms and add functionality to their websites. Notably, nearly one-quarter of state second wave laws explicitly require companies to create "Do Not Sell My Information" buttons.

---

[5]   A more comprehensive review of these bills can be found at Ari Ezra Waldman, *Privacy, Practice, and Performance*, 110 CAL. L. REV. 1221 (2022).

[6]   *See* Ariz. S. 1614 § 18–701(H); H.R. 2729, 54th Leg., 2d Reg. Sess. §§ 18–574(B), 18–577(G)(3) (Ariz. 2020).

[7]   *See* S. 2330, 101st Gen. Assemb., 1st Reg. Sess. § 35(l)(3) (Ill. 2020); S. 2263, 101st Gen. Assemb., 1st Reg. Sess. § 30(3) (Ill. 2019).

[8]   ME. REV. STAT. ANN. tit. 35-A, § 9301(3) (2020).

Requests to delete, correct, and port data also have to be evaluated. That means that companies must create internal processes for verifying and responding to these requests, processes that include hiring privacy professionals to review user requests, tasking engineers to code new functionality, and developing an internal reporting structure for approving, rejecting, and even appealing decisions. Therefore, as second wave privacy laws on the books establish individual rights to data, they are also creating corporate practices for implementing and evaluating those rights.

4.2 Compliance

This is the other side of the two-sided coin of second wave privacy law. In addition to guaranteeing additional individual rights, second wave privacy law also relies on internal organizational structures. The FTC's 2011 consent decree with Google offered the first hints of this shift in the U.S.[9] As part of a settlement for misleading Google Buzz customers, the FTC ordered Google to create an internal privacy program, beginning a compliance-based approach in which regulators rely on internal corporate structures to implement the law in practice.[10] Google had to hire a chief privacy officer and staff, situate staff inside organizational hierarchies, complete risk analyses for new products, and develop privacy trainings. The company also had to conduct biennial assessments of that program.[11]

New proposals would create 16 different internal corporate programs, offices, and practices for privacy governance. Companies must develop a "process" for responding to user opt-out requests,[12] train their employ-

---

9   *In re* Google, Inc., No. C-4336, at 4 (F.T.C. Oct. 13, 2011), https://www.ftc .gov/sites/default/files/documents/cases/2011/10/111024googlebuzzdo.pdf (requiring a company to create a "comprehensive privacy program" for the first time).

10   Kaminski, *supra* note 3, at 1565.

11   Daniel J. Solove and Woodrow Hartzog, *The FTC and the New Common Law of Privacy*, 114 COLUM. L. REV. 583, 617-18 (2011).

12   *E.g.*, CCPA, CAL. CIV. CODE § 1798.135(a)(1) (2021); MYOBA, S. 2637, 116th Cong. §§ 6(a)(6), 7(b)(1)(D)(i)-(ii), 7(b)(1)(F) (2019) (requiring consumer consent, consumer access, and correction by the covered entity if a consumer's personal information is inaccurate); H.R. 216, 2021 Leg., Reg.

ees on privacy issues,[13] keep records on data collected,[14] and complete impact assessments when developing new products.[15] They have to develop "organizational" measures, like comprehensive privacy programs, to ensure compliance and conduct regular audits—both of processors and vendors and of the privacy programs themselves.[16] A proposal

---

Sess. §§ 9(a)(1)-(2) (Ala. 2021); H. 3910, 102d Gen. Assemb., 1st Reg. Sess. § 40(a)(1)-(2) (Ill. 2021); S. 46, 192d Gen. Ct., Reg. Sess. § 3(c)(1) (Mass. 2021); S. 569, 2021 Gen. Assemb., 2021 Sess. § 75-72(b)-(c) (N.C. 2021); S. 6701, 2021 Leg., 244th Reg. Sess. § 1102(9) (N.Y. 2021); S. 5062, 67th Leg., Reg. Sess. §§ 103(2)-(5) (Wash. 2021); S. 1614, 54th Leg., 2d Reg. Sess. § 18-701(L)(1)-(4) (Ariz. 2020); S. 2330, 101st Gen. Assemb., 1st Reg. Sess. § 30(a) (Ill. 2020); H. 5603, 101st Gen. Assemb., 2d Reg. Sess. § 40(a)(1)-(2) (Ill. 2020); H. 784, 2020 Gen. Assemb., 441st Sess. § 14-4204 (Md. 2020); H. 1656, 2020 Gen. Assemb., 441st Sess. § 14-4204 (Md. 2020); H.R. 3936, 91st Leg., 2d Reg. Sess § 325O.05 subdiv. 2 (Minn. 2020); A. 3255, 219th Leg., 1st Ann. Sess. § 8 (N.J. 2020); S. 418, 30th Leg., Reg. Sess. § 487J-H (Haw. 2019); H. 1253, 2019 Leg., 2019 Reg. Sess. § 9(a)-(b) (Miss. 2019).

[13]   *E.g.*, CCPA § 1798.135(a)(3); CDPSA, S. 1494, 117th Cong. § 6(c)(2)(A) (2021); COPRA, S. 2968, 116th Cong. § 107(b)(4) (2019); Ariz. S. 1614 § 18-701(L)(5); Ill. H. 5603 § 40(a)(6); Md. H. 784 § 14-4204(E); Md. H. 1656 § 14-4204(E); Haw. S. 418 § 487J-H(6); S. 176, 54th Leg., 1st Sess. § 6 (N.M. 2019).

[14]   *E.g.*, MYOBA § 6(a)(2)(A); Online Privacy Act of 2019, H.R. 4978, 116th Cong. § 202(b) (2019); Haw. S. 418 § 487J-H (requiring lists of identifying information collected).

[15]   *E.g.*, Virginia Consumer Data Protection Act, § 59.1-580; CDPSA § 6(b) (3); SAFE DATA Act, S. 4626, 116th Cong. § 107(a)(1), (b) (2020); MYOBA § 7(b)(G)-(H); S. 190, 73d Gen. Assemb., 1st Reg. Sess. § 6-1-1309 (Colo. 2021); S. 893, 2021 Gen. Assemb., Jan. Sess. § 7(a) (Conn. 2021); N.C. S. 569 § 75-74; N.Y. S. 6701 § 1103(b); Wash. S. 5062 § 109; Ill. S. 2330 § 35(l); Minn. H.R. 3936 § 325O.08; H.D. 473, 2020 Gen. Assemb., Reg. Sess. § 59.1-576 (Va. 2020); S. 2263, 101st Gen. Assemb., 1st Reg. Sess. § 30 (Ill. 2019); H.R. 4390, 86th Leg., Reg. Sess. § 541.058 (Tex. 2019) (establishing an accountability program to assess risk); *see also* Kaminski, *supra* note 3, at 1603–05 (noting that PIAs are internal documents meant to help balance risks and benefits and intended to keep privacy front of mind during design).

[16]   On setting up privacy programs: *E.g.*, COPRA §§ 201 & 202(b)(1) (requiring privacy professionals involved and responsible for compliance to implement comprehensive privacy programs and internal reporting structures); MYOBA §§ 6(a)(7), 7(b)(1)(A)-(B) (requiring organizational measures to protect privacy including biennial review of information provided to consumers for exercising opt out requests); Privacy Bill of Rights, S. 1214, 116th Cong. § 13(a)(1) (2019); Minn. H.R. 3936 § 325O.04(b)(1) (requiring processors to have organizational measures to assist data controller with com-

in Minnesota would require an internal appeals process and four other laws discuss independent tests and annual impact assessments of automated processing or facial recognition.[17] The Mind Your Own Business Act requires companies to develop an internal process to track opt-out requests of consumers with whom they are not in a direct relationship but nevertheless hold their data.[18]

Several laws call for companies to hire or designate at least one privacy officer.[19] Many proposals require companies to develop internal processes for ensuring that third-party vendors comply with the law.[20] Two laws require executive attestations and certifications of compliance.[21] And the SAFE DATA Act calls on a "professional standards body" to write its own rules that, if followed, would constitute compliance with the law.[22]

Reliance on these internal structures of compliance reflects the decades-long trend toward "collaborative governance" or "new governance".[23] Based on scholarship in the field of public administration, new governance emphasized what scholars called "agile," devolved, and informal models of policymaking and enforcement, including best practices and industry guidances, instead of top-down "command and control" regulation.[24] It is an approach to regulation that relies on a partnership between public authorities and private actors to achieve regulatory goals.[25]

---

pliance). On audits: *E.g.*, COPRA § 202(b)(2); MYOBA § 5(a)(1); Minn. H.R. 3936 § 3250.04(d)(3).

[17] Minn. H. 3936 §§ 3250.05 subdiv. 3, 3250.085(a) (requiring an internal appeals process and independent tests of facial recognition).

[18] MYOBA § 6(a)(4).

[19] *E.g.*, CDPSA §§ 6(c)(1), 7(b); SAFE DATA Act § 301(a)-(b); COPRA § 202(a)(1)-(2); MYOBA § 7(b)(C); Privacy Bill of Rights § 14; GDPR, arts. 28, 39(1)(b).

[20] *E.g.*, Data Care Act of 2021, S. 919, 117th Cong. § 3(b)(3)(C) (2021); COPRA § 203(c)(1)(A)-(B); MYOBA § 6(a)(8); Privacy Bill of Rights § 10; Tex. H.R. 4390 § 541.059.

[21] COPRA § 201; MYOBA § 5(b).

[22] SAFE DATA Act §§ 206(c), 404(a).

[23] Jody Freeman, *Collaborative Governance in the Administrative State*, 45 U.C.L.A. L. Rev. 1 (1997).

[24] Jody Freeman, The Private Role in Public Governance, 75 N.Y.U. L. Rev. 543 (2000); Orly Lobel, The Renew Deal: The Fall of Regulation and the Rise of Governance in Contemporary Legal Thought, 89 Minn. L. Rev. 342 (2004).

[25] Kaminski, *supra* note 3, at 1599.

Collaborative governance at its best is "a highly tailored, site-calibrated regulatory system that aims to pull inputs from, obtain buy-in from, and affect the internal institutional structures and decision-making heuristics of the private sector" while maintaining popular legitimacy and achieving better social welfare outcomes.[26] In the privacy space, collaborative governance is meant to supplement privacy's traditional reliance on transparency, notice, and consent.

In collaborative governance, the government plays the role of a "backdrop threat" that encourages private sector engagement, convenes regulated entities and civil society together, certifies compliance protocols, and, if necessary, enforces the law when things go awry. Private actors develop the systems of compliance on their own with the government as a top-down regulator.[27] To ensure accountability, collaborative governance relies on negotiated settlements, safe harbors, codes of conduct, audits, informal delegation of interpretation authority to private actors, impact assessments, ongoing self-monitoring, and incentives for private ordering in the public interest. The goal is to keep sufficient flexibility in the legal system so regulated entities will want to participate and to ensure companies do so in the public good.[28]

Proponents see several benefits to the collaborative model. Public-private partnerships bring private sector expertise to governance, which may be especially necessary in the complex and highly digitized information economy.[29] Technological development also moves fast, so the collaborative governance model offers "an ongoing, iterative system of monitoring and compliance" in place of the long, drawn-out process of administrative rulemaking. The model also enhances industry buy-in and perceived legitimacy by giving regulated entities a seat at the table and enabling them to help regulators craft workable solutions.[30] In short, there are reasons collaborative governance is so popular.

---

[26]   Id. at 1560. See also Dennis Hirsch, Going Dutch? Collaborative Dutch Privacy Regulation and the Lessons it Holds for U.S. Privacy Law, 2103 MICH. ST. L. REV. 83, 99-102; W. Nicholson Price, Regulating Black-Box Medicine, 116 MICH. L. REV. 421, 465-71 (2017).

[27]   Kaminski, supra note 3, at 1561–62.

[28]   Id. at 1564–67.

[29]   KENNETH BAMBERGER AND DEIRDRE MULLIGAN, PRIVACY ON THE GROUND 12-13 (2015).

[30]   Kaminski, supra note 3, at 1562.

This shift to compliance is also part of what sociolegal scholars call the "managerialization of law," or the "infusion of managerial or business values and ideas into law."[31] Second wave privacy law explicitly envisions that compliance professionals—privacy professionals, privacy lawyers, and other compliance experts—will bring the law into their organizations, translate its requirements for their bosses, and implement it throughout the company.[32] The second wave seeks management of data up and down the line to keep privacy in mind during collection and processing.[33] But along with that shift in responsibility comes the "reconceptualization of law so that it is more consistent with general principles of good management."[34] Theoretically, managerialism is agnostic as to legal values; good management is not necessarily in conflict with the underlying purpose of social legislation. But managerialism does give regulated entities themselves—the intermediaries between the laws on the books and the people those laws are meant to protect—unique power to define what the law means in practice.

4.3   Origins of the second wave

It is pretty remarkable that, outside of some marginal differences (in terms of emphasis, which rights are protected, and which compliance requirements are included), most of these proposals look similar. They add a combination of individual rights of control and internal compliance structures (the rights-compliance model to the traditional model of privacy notices and consent buttons). This means that policymakers seem committed (or stuck on) a single model for privacy governance.

This uniformity is notable, as is policymakers' coalescence around this particular model. It is unusual for policymakers in a country as politically polarized as the U.S. is right now to roughly agree on a single framework for new privacy laws. After all, there are other options. The choice of the

---

[31]   LAUREN EDELMAN, WORKING LAW: COURTS, CORPORATIONS, AND SYMBOLIC CIVIL RIGHTS 25 (2016).

[32]   See Kaminski, *supra* note 3, at 1559–60.

[33]   See *id.* at 1561.

[34]   EDELMAN, *supra* note 31, at 25-6; *see* JULIE E. COHEN, BETWEEN TRUTH AND POWER: LEGAL CONSTRUCTIONS OF INFORMATIONAL CAPITALISM 144-45 (2019).

rights-compliance model is even more surprising given that scholars generally agree that employing this framework, which may work elsewhere, in the U.S. regulatory context is quite risky.[35]

These second wave practices did not just emerge out of thin air. They had to come from somewhere, and the rough uniformity has to be explained by some common threads, pressures, and influences. Legal scholar Anu Bradford suggested that a "Brussels Effect" would make all privacy laws accord with those of the E.U.[36] Bradford predicted that multinational companies would voluntarily adopt EU rules like the GDPR, in part, because of the EU's unique combination of market power and regulatory capacity. And since data flows are difficult to constrain within political boundaries, Bradford reasoned that companies in the information industry will be uniquely susceptible to EU regulatory power. EU law also bans data transfers from the EU to other countries if those countries do not have "adequate" data protection laws. Therefore, Bradford predicted that industry and governments would strengthen their practices to meet EU demands.[37] However, Anupam Chander, Margot Kaminski, and Bill McGeveran rightly note that the EU has had a privacy law for decades—the EU Privacy Directive came into effect in 1995, and it did not spur Congress or the states to act. They suggest that it was the legal entrepreneurship of leading privacy advocates in California who took advantage of that state's unique lawmaking process that catalyzed the explosion of recent privacy proposals in the U.S.[38]

Implicit in Bradford's argument is a formalistic distinction between law and society. Bradford looked to a law-on-the-books catalyst for other laws on the books, conceptualizing law as an autonomous institution off on its own. But that's not how it works. The relationship between law and society is a reciprocal one: Law reflects and influences social change, whether it be changes in the family or shifts to an industrial or information economy. To think the law is only influenced by other law is to ignore society's role.

---

[35]   Woodrow Hartzog and Neil Richards, *Privacy's Constitutional Moment and the Limits of Data Protection*, 61 B.C. L. Rev. 1687, 1714, 1721–37 (2020).

[36]   Anu Bradford, *The Brussels Effect*, 107 Nw. U. L. Rev. 1, 22–26 (2012).

[37]   *Id.* at 10–19, 24–26.

[38]   Anupam Chander, Margot Kaminski, and Bill McGeveran, *Catalyzing Privacy Law*, 105 Minn. L. Rev. 1733, 1737-38 (2021).

There are other limitations to the conventional wisdom's focus on the GDPR's or the CCPA's influence. Some scholars put considerable faith in the norm entrepreneurship of a small group of privacy advocates who forced the California legislature's hand in 2018 but neglected to consider what companies were already doing internally by that time.[39] These scholars recognize that the rights/compliance model was not invented by the CCPA, but insufficiently account for how that makes the narrative more complex. Privacy law-as-compliance in the U.S. dates as far back as 2011, when the FTC first required Google to develop a "comprehensive privacy program."[40] Individual rights to access, restrict processing, and correction are even older; they were part of the original Code of Fair Information Practice recommended by HEW in 1973.[41] As such, they predate every EU privacy law (and even the EU itself). Chander, Kaminski, and McGeveran also do not characterize recent privacy proposals as a mix of rights and compliance, instead seeing them as primarily rights based.[42] But that can't be right. Compliance is a critical piece of these proposals when viewed from the perspective of practice. Even a proposal that simply allows individuals to access and delete their data requires companies to create internal processes to intake, assess, respond to, and implement those requests.

Plus, neither the formalist nor realist theory explains why policymakers and advocates agreed on *these* proposals. There are lots of other options. Policymakers could have taken Woodrow Hartzog's advice and used various legal tools to ensure that privacy protections and anti-manipulation guarantees are designed into new technology products.[43] They could have banned certain types of data collection. They could have even done nothing. They didn't; they all chose individual rights and compliance-based governance.

---

[39]   *Id.*

[40]   Agreement Containing Consent Order at 6, *In re* Google, Inc., Docket No. C-4336, No. 102 3136 (F.T.C. Oct. 24, 2011) [hereinafter Google Consent Decree], https://www.ftc.gov/sites/default/files/documents/cases/2011/10/111024googlebuzzdo.pdf.

[41]   U.S. Dep't of Health, Educ., & Welfare, No. (OS)73-94, Records, Computers, and the Rights of Citizens: Report of the Secretary's Advisory Committee on Automated Personal Data Systems 8-15 (1973), https://aspe.hhs.gov/report/records-computers-and-rights-citizens.

[42]   Chandar, Kaminski, and McGeveran, *supra* note 38, at 1737–38.

[43]   Woodrow Hartzog, Privacy's Blueprint (2019).

Perhaps policymakers are risk averse or lack imagination. Perhaps we are all steeped in the same governing discourses that define how we think about privacy, leading policymakers to adopt similar ideas that do not upset traditional structures of power. Political scientists might explain the similarities by pointing to the Overton Window, or the theory that only a small set of policy options are acceptable in any given political moment.[44]

I think there is a different explanation. Recent privacy proposals follow a rights/compliance approach because the second wave's practices—industry input in regulations, settlements and consent decrees, self-audits, PIAs, recordkeeping, codes of conduct, privacy offices, and privacy self-navigation—are long-standing practices that industry developed over time.[45] As a result, the routinization of these practices socially constructed privacy law from the ground up. Most state and federal proposals would codify social practices of privacy that regulators, industry, and individuals have been engaged in for some time, long before the GDPR and the CCPA. The repetition of these performances may have normalized them, acculturating stakeholders to think that this is what privacy law is and should be. Policymakers could not think of other options because performances of privacy on the ground had already created the category of privacy law for them.

4.4   The political economy of the first and second waves

The previous sections clarified some of the practical developments in privacy law and where they came from. First wave privacy law walled off the information industry from government intervention. Indeed, notice-and-consent was originally developed as a way to stave off potentially more robust regulation that could threaten the industry's innovation

---

[44]   The Overton Window, MACKINAC CTR. PUB. POL'Y, https://www.mackinac.org/.
[45]   Ari Ezra Waldman, *Privacy, Practice, and Performance*, 110 CAL. L. REV. 1221, 1233-251 (2022).

imperative.[46] The first wave was also premised on notions of autonomy, liberty, and freedom. As one leading scholar noted, "[p]roviding people with notice, access, and the ability to control their data is key to facilitating some autonomy in a world where decisions are increasingly being made about them with the use of personal data."[47] The first wave put the onus of privacy navigation on the user, making the agreement between users and data collectors on the terms of a privacy policy the locus of the law's concern.[48] Policy reforms to hold platforms more accountable were attacked as "break[ing] the internet" and undermining a growing market of e-commerce and social media.[49] Therefore, the first wave arguably reflected a "hands off," or classically liberal, approach to law and the information economy.

The second wave is different. As we have seen, its practices are largely about compliance, including reliance on industry best practices, impact assessments, audits, and privacy offices that manage, rather than restrict, data use. These governance mechanisms are managerial in that they integrate management values like efficiency into organizational decision-making and rely on professionals to make those decisions in ways that accord with good management.[50] The second wave represents a choice to filter privacy law through corporate compliance and to manage data collection and processing from within. By using internal and managerialized corporate structures to do regulatory work, second wave practices reflect a neoliberal approach.[51]

---

[46]   Solove and Hartzog, supra note 11, at 592–94; see also Michael D. Scott, The FTC, the Unfairness Doctrine, and Data Security Breach Litigation: Has the Commission Gone Too Far?, 60 ADMIN. L. REV. 127, 130-31 (2008); Steven Hetcher, The FTC as Internet Privacy Norm Entrepreneur, 53 VAND. L. REV. 2041, 2046-47 (2000).

[47]   Daniel J. Solove, Introduction: Privacy Self-Management and the Consent Dilemma, 126 HARV. L. REV. 1880, 1899 (2013).

[48]   David Singh Grewal and Jedediah Purdy, Introduction: Law and Neoliberalism, 77 L. & CONTEMP. PROBS. 1, 13 (2014).

[49]   Danielle Citron and Benjamin Wittes, The Internet Will Not Break: Denying Bad Samaritans § 230 Immunity, 86 FORDHAM L. REV. 401, 401 (2017).

[50]   See Cohen, supra note 34, at 144–45.

[51]   See id. at 7; David Harvey, Neoliberalism as Creative Destruction, 610 ANNALS OF AM. ACAD. POL. & SOC. SCI. 21, 21-22 (2007). The term "neoliberalism" is admittedly overused and can be confusing. See JAMIE PECK, CONSTRUCTIONS OF NEOLIBERAL REASON 15 (2010); Terry Flew,

Classical liberalism and neoliberalism share some common elements, as their names suggest. They both "assert[] and defen[d] ... economic power against political intervention."[52] But where classical liberalism envisions a consistently *laissez faire* relationship between law and markets, neoliberalism advocates for a state that is thoroughly infused with market thinking—a belief that the market is the best way to advance social welfare, and that only market-based options are workable.[53] Neoliberal governance can be interventionist or noninterventionist, but it is always infused with market values. Such market-based thinking includes valorizing efficiency in institutions, focusing on wealth maximization of private actors, minimizing transaction costs, using cost-benefit analyses to make decisions,[54] and relying on law to intervene to protect those values.[55]

Neoliberal assumptions about the relationship between law and markets, the role of efficiency in governance, and the role of regulators pervade second wave privacy law. For instance, second wave privacy law treats privacy as a field of law that is "about the market," in which the quest for efficiency becomes a descriptive and normative goal of the law.[56] Even in its ideal form, the rights-compliance model is supposed to take the "benefits of self-regulation without its pitfalls" while still offering the possibility of "better approximat[ing] a market-driven optimum."[57] The Brookings Institution, which has released its own proposal for a second wave law, implicitly adopted this assumption in its proposed legislative findings as well, noting that law has to evolve "as technology, innovation, and services — and risks to privacy — evolve."[58] This view perpetuates overlapping discourses, taken as a given among many policymakers

---

Michel Foucault's The Birth of Biopolitics *and Contemporary Neo-liberalism Debates*, 108 THESIS ELEVEN 44, 44-45 (2012).

[52]   Grewal and Purdy, *supra* note 48, at 1.

[53]   *See id.* at 6, 13–14; *see also* Jamie Peck and Adam Tickell, *Conceptualizing Neoliberalism, Thinking Thatcherism, in* CONTESTING NEOLIBERALISM: URBAN FRONTIERS 26, 33 (Helga Leitner et al. eds., 2007).

[54]   *See* Jedediah Britton-Purdy, David Singh Grewal, Amy Kapczynski and K. Sabeel Rahman, *Building a Law-and-Political-Economy Framework: Beyond the Twentieth-Century Synthesis*, 129 YALE L.J.1796-1800, 1812 (2020).

[55]   *See* Grewal and Purdy, *supra* note 48, at 6; Britton-Purdy et al., *supra* note 54, at1784, 1796–1800.

[56]   Britton-Purdy et al., *supra* note 54, at 1790.

[57]   Kaminski, *supra* note 3, at 1561.

[58]   Cameron F. Kerry and John B. Morris, *Framing a Privacy Right: Legislative Findings for Federal Privacy Legislation*, BROOKINGS INST. (Dec. 8, 2020),

today, that innovation is normatively good, regulation is normatively bad, the two are in tension, and the market is the ideal.[59]

Compliance requirements like privacy impact assessments also reflect neoliberalism's primacy in second wave privacy law. Even though PIAs are supposed to "identif[y] and evaluate[] potential threats to individual privacy ... [and] the appropriate risk mitigation measures," they are often recast to incorporate the profit-seeking interests of industry. They evaluate risks to the company of reduced profit or litigation without considering the privacy risks of consumers.[60] In practice, PIAs also tend to boil down to cost-benefit analyses. Practitioners admit this. The Future of Privacy Forum (FPF) published a guide explicitly for the purpose of helping "organizations in their weighing of the benefits of new or expanded data processing against attendant privacy risks."[61] Other practitioners have identified "benefit-risk analysis" as one of five components of data stewardship.[62]

Other second wave practices also integrate market values. Many companies outsource some of their privacy compliance functions to technology vendors, hoping to achieve efficiencies and reduce costs.[63] Granted,

---

[59] https://www.brookings.edu/research/framing-a-privacy-right-legislative-findings-for-federal-privacy-legislation/.
See, e.g., Consumer Perspectives: Policy Principles for a Federal Data Privacy Framework in the United States: Hearing Before the S. Comm. on Commerce, Sci., & Transp., 116th Cong. (2019) (statement of Sen. Maria Cantwell, Chair, S. Comm. On Commerce, Sci. & Transp.).

[60] EDELMAN, supra note 31, at 77-99; Ari Ezra Waldman, Privacy Law's False Promise, 97 WASH. U. L. REV. 773, 789-803 (2020).

[61] Jules Polonetsky, Omer Tene and Joseph Jerome, Future of Privacy Forum, Benefit-Risk Analysis for Big Data Projects 1 (2014), https://dataanalytics.report/Resources/Whitepapers/aa942e84-9174-4dbe-b4cc-911bff14daf8_FPF_DataBenefitAnalysis_FINAL.pdf.

[62] Kelsey Finch and Omer Tene, Smart Cities: Privacy, Transparency and Community, in THE CAMBRIDGE HANDBOOK OF CONSUMER PRIVACY 125, 130-31 (Evan Selinger et al. eds., 2018); see also Ira S. Rubinstein and Bilyana Petkova, Governing Privacy in the Datafied City, 47 FORDHAM URB. L. J. 755, 791-92 (2020).

[63] See COHEN, supra note 34, at 156-57; Ari Ezra Waldman, Outsourcing Privacy, 96 NOTRE DAME L. REV. REFLECTION 194, 195-96 (2021); IAPP & TrustArc, MEASURING PRIVACY OPERATIONS 7-8, 11 (2018), https://iapp.org/media/pdf/resource_center/IAPP-Measuring-Privacy-Operations-FINAL.pdf-Measuring-Privacy-Operations-FINAL.pdf.

outsourcing is not required by any of the second wave's provisions, but its proliferation highlights the second wave's managerialism and proceduralism: when legal compliance means checking boxes and filling out forms, it is easy to shift those responsibilities off campus.[64] Second wave laws empower industry to set its own codes of conduct and standards, certify compliance with those standards, and rely on certification as a safe harbor to introduce the needs and preferences of market actors in determining legal compliance.[65] FTC regulators are on the record supporting compliance safe harbors, as well.[66]

What is more, second wave rights of control, all of which have to be exercised by individuals through affirmative requests, reflect neoliberalism's concern with providing "equal enjoyment of unfettered choice" to consumers and the normative argument that individual choices in the market is the fastest route to general welfare.[67] More importantly, it reflects neoliberalism's ideological preference for reducing legal interests to individual claims subject to individual remedies: access to my data, correcting my data, objecting to the processing of my data.[68] Understood in this way, the second wave is decidedly neoliberal. That should come as no surprise. Neoliberal managerialism is what passes for regulation in the U.S. Julie Cohen argues that the legal institutions of informational capitalism as a whole are decidedly managerial.[69] They rely on audits and compliance tools as hollowed out public institutions turn to industry to self-certify their compliance with the law.[70] The practical content of the GDPR, the CCPA, and their second wave cousins is similar.

---

[64]   See RONAN McIVOR, THE OUTSOURCING PROCESS: STRATEGIES FOR EVALUATION AND MANAGEMENT 40-59 (2005).

[65]   See, e.g., SAFE DATA Act, S. 4626, 116th Cong. §§206(c)(3), 404(a) (2019); see also Kaminski, supra note 3, at 1574; Orly Lobel, The Renew Deal: The Fall of Regulation and the Rise of Governance in Con- temporary Legal Thought, 89 MINN. L. REV. 342, 375, 389, 392 (2004).

[66]   Redressing Privacy Violations: A Conversation with Experts, UNIV. OF WASH. TECH POLICY LAB & MICROSOFT (Dec. 10, 2020), https://medius .studios.ms/Embed/video-nc/CELAReadress-2020 (comments by former FTC Commissioners Brill and McSweeney).

[67]   Grewal and Purdy, supra note 48, at 13.

[68]   Neoliberalism is centered on "the consenting individual" as "the author of the norms under which she will live." Britton-Purdy et al., supra note 54, at 1814–15.

[69]   COHEN, supra note 34, at 144-45.

[70]   See id. at 192–93.

4.5   The meaning of privacy in the second wave

Nearly 20 years ago, Daniel Solove argued that the salient problem with private intermediaries and governments amassing digital dossiers about citizens is the loss of individual control over personal information.[71] Collecting data that are already available or required for doing business, Solove argues, does not injure personal privacy in the conventional sense; that is, there is no "discrete wrong" that occurs through the behavior of some "particular wrongdoer" who, say, discloses personal information to the media.[72] Rather, the problem is structural. Data are collected without sufficient controls, so Solove recommends a new architecture of data collection that "affords people greater participation in the uses of their information."[73] He recommended starting at the FIPPs, the very recommendations from the HEW that undergirded privacy law's first wave.[74] At their core, these recommendations aim at shifting control over data from the collector (an intermediary or a government agency) back to the source of that information (the individual).

This vision—privacy-as-control (as opposed to privacy-as-choice)—sits at the core of the second wave of privacy law. Privacy-as-control is the idea that we should be able to have some power over what happens with our data, even after initially giving up or consenting to its extraction. Therefore, if privacy-as-choice manifested in the form of privacy policies and consent buttons, privacy-as-control manifests as consent buttons, links to access and download all the data a platform has about a user, deletion buttons, "Do Not Sell My Information" requests, as well as other self-management tools that give people more ways to intentionally navigate the collection and use of their data.

Yes, that is different than simple (and illusory) consent. But, as I argue in the next chapter, the differences are barely an inch wide and a millimeter deep. Privacy-as-control and its second wave of privacy law are far more similar to privacy-as-choice and its first wave of privacy than most people would have you believe.

---

[71]   DANIEL SOLOVE, THE DIGITAL PERSON 90 (2004).
[72]   Id..at 94.
[73]   Id. at 102–03.
[74]   Id. at 104.

5   The weaknesses of
        individual privacy rights

Anyone even remotely familiar with either privacy scholarship or privacy law practice cannot reasonably think notice-and-consent is sufficient. So, the second wave added additional rights. Perhaps additional affirmative rights of access, correction, and deletion will somehow change corporate manipulative, predatory, and extractive behavior. I'm not so sure. In other words, will the part of the second wave focused on individual privacy rights of control, as its been described in Chapter 4, make a difference?

Some people think so.[1] They believe that some individual rights of control are better than nothing. They (rightly) believe that, in general, the perfect should not be the enemy of the good. I argue that the second wave rights/compliance model will have little to no positive effect on our privacy, and the next two chapters explain why. In fact, they may make things worse by entrenching data extraction forever.

Rights, like visibility, are traps.[2] Individual rights of control require an infrastructure to make them meaningful, and that infrastructure does not

---

[1]   *See, e.g.*, Margot E. Kaminski, *The Case for Data Privacy Rights (or, Please, a Little Optimism)*, 97 NOTRE DAME L. REV. REFLECTION 385, 386 (2022) (arguing that the despite the flaws of "[g]rounding data privacy law in individual rights," individual rights nonetheless serve various purposes including reflecting common understandings of privacy and defense against First Amendment challenges, among other goals); Mike Hintze, *In Defense of the Long Privacy Statement*, 76 MD. L. REV. 1044, 1045 (2017) (suggesting the value of privacy statements is in informing consumers of their rights and choices).

[2]   MICHEL FOUCAULT, DISCIPLINE AND PUNISH 200 (Alan Sheridan trans., Vintage Books 2d ed. 1995) (1977). The famous sentence—"[v]isibility is a trap"—comes from Foucault's discussion of the panoptic prison, which replaced the traditional dungeon's darkness with full light so prison guards

exist in the law of informational capitalism.[3] Nor does any piece of privacy legislation currently under consideration create that infrastructure. This chapter offers five critiques of the primacy of individual rights in privacy laws. First, the social critique focuses on the mismatch between individual rights and the social nature of data in informational capitalism. When rights are the primary tools in a regulatory model for data-extractive capitalism, our coordinated subordination is ignored. Second, a behavioral critique argues that people are, for the most part, incapable of exercising their individual rights. When privacy law focuses on rights, little will change on the ground because few of us will be able to exercise those rights. Third, a practical critique demonstrates how even those who support individual rights of control implicitly recognize that rights only have real power with structural reform. When rights are primary regulatory tools in privacy, those rights cannot overcome preexisting legal and technical barriers to effective enforcement. Fourth, an expressive critique challenges the message of individual responsibility sent by rights-based laws. Individual rights-focused privacy laws perpetuate the idea that privacy is our problem alone to manage. It isn't and it shouldn't be. Fifth, and finally, a structural critique argues that when we use individual rights to solve structural problems, we miss the underlying injustices. The balance of this chapter treats each critique in order.

5.1   The social critique

The information economy is a social economy. Decisions to consent to data collection are never purely personal decisions. Instead, one person's decision to consent to sharing their information frequently implicates others sharing some sort of connection with them. The most obvious example of this is when a family member decides to send their saliva to 23andMe to map their DNA. By doing so, they share information about everyone who shares their DNA (parents, sisters, children, and so forth).

---

can maintain watch over prisoners at all times. The legibility of the prisoner at all times reduced the prisoner's freedom even more. *Id.*

[3]   Informational capitalism describes a political and economic system in which the means of production are oriented toward the extraction of value from data and information. Julie E. Cohen, Between Truth and Power: Legal Constructions of Informational Capitalism 5–6 (2019).

In a social economy, individual rights do not control what happens with our data. This is the social critique of individual rights.

In fact, the "sociality" of data is the core feature of the information economy.[4] That is, information about one person doesn't just affect that person; it affects everyone like them. Producers extract profit from data specifically because data collected about one person help them make inferences about other people.[5] If I purchase several books about the history of Paris or buy in-home exercise equipment, retailers and platforms can assess my latent characteristics (age, education, income, location, sexual orientation, relationship status, you name it) and target others with similar characteristics with advertisements for another book about Paris (or maybe Lyon or Marsailles) or an indoor exercise bicycle, new running shoes, or a yoga mat.

This puts us all in data relationships with each other that individual rights—which we alone can exercise against data collectors—entirely ignore.[6] A person wrongfully arrested because a facial recognition algorithm identified them as a suspect is socially connected with the person whose voluntarily uploaded picture was used to train the facial recognition tool. Critically, although the individual arrested certainly has a privacy interest in the collection, use, and processing of data related to their face, that interest is independent of the interests of the person who uploaded the picture, thereby starting the causal chain of picture, collection, processing, training artificial intelligence, misidentification, and arrest. The victim's privacy interest—and their interest in not being wrongfully swept up into a biased criminal justice system—is simply not represented in the relationship between the uploader and the host platform. And yet that "vertical" relationship between uploader and platform is the only one even remotely mediated by individual rights.[7]

---

4   Salomé Viljoen, *A Relational Theory of Data Governance*, 131 YALE L.J. 573, 582 (2021).
5   *Id.* at 610–11.
6   Daniel J. Solove, *The Limitations of Privacy Rights*, 98 NOTRE DAME L. REV. 975 (2023).
7   Viljoen, *supra* note 4, at 607–09 (describing data governance's response to downstream social effects from data collection as "unsatisfying" because of its commitment to individualism despite the known "horizontal," or population-based, nature of data flows).

Therefore, a central feature of an individual rights approach to privacy law is its complete disregard for how an inherently social, inference-based economy actually functions.[8] It expresses a narrow, radically individuated property interest in data that has limited value and limited reach.

5.2   The behavioral critique

I suppose it is possible that if enough of us exercise our individual rights to delete, port, and opt out of tracking, things might change. We could conceivably starve the information industry of the materials and labor it needs to extract population-level insights from individual users. But much social science evidence suggests that this will never happen. This is the behavioral critique of individual privacy rights.

As we discussed in Chapter 3, individual rights of control presume human rationality. The right to opt out of tracking is contingent on individuals' ability to understand how they are being tracked and the effects of that tracking. It then requires individuals to process that knowledge, align it with their privacy preferences, and make the choice to opt out or consent. But humans are not perfectly rational beings; at best, our rationality is bounded.[9] More likely, our rationality is malleable.[10] If policymakers expect people to exercise their individual rights in any appreciable numbers, they will likely be disappointed.

Individuals must overcome all sorts of biases that cause them to pump the brakes on acting, let alone acting rationally. We face status quo biases that make us more comfortable with maintaining things as they are.[11] We face problems of overchoice, where the sheer number of choices and steps

---

[8] Alicia Solow-Niederman, *Information Privacy and the Inference Economy*, 117 Nw. U. L. Rev. 357, 401, 404 (2022).

[9] Alessandro Acquisti and Jens Grossklags, *What Can Behavioral Economics Teach Us About Privacy*, in Digital Privacy: Theory, Technologies, and Practices 363, 369–70 (Alessandro Acquisti et al. eds., 2008).

[10] *See generally* Stephanie Plamondon Bair, *Malleable Rationality*, 79 Ohio St. L.J. 17 (2018) (arguing that rationality changes due to time, experience, and policy).

[11] William Samuelson and Richard Zeckhauser, *Status Quo Bias in Decision Making*, 1 J. Risk & Uncertainty 7, 8 (1988).

we must take to opt out of cookies creates paralysis.[12] We are also prone to hyperbolic discounting, or the tendency to overweigh the immediate consequences of a decision and to underweigh those consequences that may occur in the future.[13]

Data tracking often carries with it certain immediate benefits— convenience, access, or social engagement, to name just a few. But individuals usually do not immediately feel its costs, whether the intangible costs of risk and anxiety or the delayed costs of identity theft and loss of autonomy.[14] Therefore, our tendency to overvalue current rewards while inadequately discounting the cost of future risks makes us much less likely to exercise our right to opt out. Our disclosure decisions are also subject to framing biases, especially when platforms describe opting out of tracking as being harmful: "If you don't allow cookies, website functionality will be diminished," or, "Opting into data collection will enable new and easier functionality."[15]

At the same time, platforms are free to manipulate these choices however they want. Sure, they can place a hyperlink to "Access My Data" somewhere on a webpage, but they can use design tricks to obscure it, redirect us, and manipulate behavior.[16] As a sociotechnical process, design includes "processes that create consumer technologies and the results of their creative process instantiated in hardware and software."[17] The field

---

[12]   See Benjamin Scheibehenne, Rainer Greifeneder and Peter M. Todd, *Can There Ever Be Too Many Options? A Meta-Analytic Review of Choice Overload*, 37 J. CONSUMER RSCH. 409, 409 (2010).

[13]   Ari Ezra Waldman, *Cognitive Biases, Dark Patterns, and the 'Privacy Paradox'*, 31 CURRENT OP. PSYCH. 105, 106 (2020); *see also* Solove, *supra* note 6 (manuscript at 10–12) (discussing how privacy rights are not meaningful if individuals do not have the time or knowledge to invoke them with respect to their data).

[14]   See Daniel J. Solove and Danielle Keats Citron, *Risk and Anxiety: A Theory of Data-Breach Harms*, 96 TEX. L. REV. 737, 756–60 (2018); Danielle Keats Citron and Daniel J. Solove, *Privacy Harms*, 102 B.U. L. REV. 793, 830–61 (2022).

[15]   Idris Adjerid, Alessandro Acquisti, Laura Brandimarte and George Loewenstein, *Sleights of Privacy: Framing, Disclosures, and the Limits of Transparency*, SOUPS '13: PROC. 9TH SYMP. ON USABLE PRIV. & SEC. 1, 10 (2013).

[16]   Waldman, *supra* note 13, at 107.

[17]   WOODROW HARTZOG, PRIVACY'S BLUEPRINT 11 (2018).

of science and technology studies has long recognized that the design of built environments constrains human behavior.[18] The same is true online, and even more so when millions, if not billions, of people with potentially different preferences are using the same service. As Woodrow Hartzog has noted, "[t]he realities of technology at scale mean that the services we use must necessarily be built in a way that constraints our choices."[19] We can only click on the buttons or select the options presented to us; we can only opt out of the options from which a website allows us to opt out.

At a minimum, the power of design means that our choices do not always reflect our real personal preferences. At worst, online platforms manipulate us into keeping the data flowing, fueling an information-hungry business model. That manipulation is often the result of so-called "dark patterns" in platform design. Dark patterns are "interface design choices that benefit an online service by coercing, steering, or deceiving users into making decisions that, if fully informed and capable of selecting alternatives, they might not make."[20] And they are common. Designers use dark patterns to hide, deceive, and goad. They confuse by asking questions in ways most people cannot understand, they obfuscate by hiding interface elements that could help protect privacy, they require registration and associated disclosures in order to access functionality, and they hide malicious behavior in the abyss of fine print. Policymakers should not expect us to act rationally when they have left in place a business model that does everything it can to trigger us to act against our own interest.

---

[18]   *See, e.g.*, Steve Woolgar, *Configuring the User: The Case of Usability Trials*, 38 Socio. Rev. 58, 59–60 (1990) (arguing that "our preconceptions about the nature and capacities of different entities shape what counts as legitimate accounts of action and behaviour" in the context of information technology).

[19]   Woodrow Hartzog, *The Case Against Idealising Control*, 4 Eur. Data Prot. L. Rev. 423, 426 (2018).

[20]   Arunesh Mathur, Gunes Acar, Michael J. Friedman, Eli Lucherini, Jonathan Mayer, Marshini Chetty and Arvind Narayanan, *Dark Patterns at Scale: Findings from a Crawl of 11K Shopping Websites*, 3 Proc. ACM on Hum.-Comput. Interaction 1, 2 (2019).

5.3   The practical critique

Cognitive limitations are not the only barriers standing in the way of us exercising our individual rights. Practical barriers also impede our privacy rights. Individual rights have no effect when rights holders cannot act on them or when they fail to hold violators accountable for their actions.

Throwing a few dollars—even a few million dollars—at state attorneys general or administrative agencies will, at most, hold a company or two accountable for the most egregious or most obvious lies and other wrongs. The leading second wave privacy law proposal in the U.S. Congress, the American Data Protection and Privacy Act, does not include any money for any enforcement mechanisms at all.[21] And even if regulators have enforcement capacity, the laws are still weak. Regulators estimate that compliance with the supposedly "stringent" law out there[22]—the California Consumer Privacy Act—will only cost $128 per business.[23] Although even proponents of individual privacy rights can see the insufficiency of rights without money for enforcement or meaningful regulation, there is a deeper problem. Rights-based privacy laws are tossing individual rights into zones of legal immunity that insulate the information industry from accountability.[24]

As we have seen, rights-based privacy laws include rights to access the information a company has about us. Some of them also include rights against discrimination. That means we can click a button, download pages and pages of data, and scour them for evidence of exclusion or mistreatment. Good luck! There are several reasons why few of us can turn that into a meaningful check on the information industry. Technical experts like computer scientists, electrical engineers, programmers, and data scientists—and those with means to pay them—are the ones most likely able to understand the data we receive. Few of us have access to

---

21   American Data Protection and Privacy Act, H.R. 8152, 117th Cong. § 401 (2022).

22   Anupam Chander, Margot E. Kaminski and William McGeveran, *Catalyzing Privacy Law*, 105 Minn. L. Rev. 1733, 1734 (2021).

23   California Privacy Protection Agency, California Consumer Privacy Act Regulations: Economic and Fiscal Impact Statement (2022).

24   Cohen, *supra* note 3 101–07.

either. The algorithms that make decisions about people's lives are protected by trade secrecy law or immunized from any kind of regulation as creative expression under the First Amendment.[25] Therefore, even if we could understand what the information industry was doing to us, too much of its business behavior is off limits from any sort of accountability.

The Supreme Court exacerbated this problem in *TransUnion LLC v. Ramirez* when it took away Congress's long-standing power to ensure that violations of acts of Congress automatically confer Article III standing.[26] The*TransUnion* case began when Ramirez and his spouse went to a car dealership to buy a car. The dealership ran a credit check through TransUnion, which incorrectly suggested that Ramirez was on a list of suspected terrorists with whom U.S. companies are not allowed to conduct business.[27] After Ramirez followed up with TransUnion, the company sent him two letters, both of which again indicated that he was a "potential match" for two different people on the terrorist watch list.[28] Ramirez sued. He argued that TransUnion failed to use "reasonable procedures" to ensure the accuracy of their credit files and yet shared that information with third parties, both in violation of the Fair Credit Reporting Act, for FCRA.[29] To increase the case's impact, Ramirez tried to bring his case as a class action representing more than 8,000 people who had received similar letters from TransUnion even though none of them were on the watch list. Only about 1,800 of them had their credit files shared with third parties.[30] The Supreme Court said that even though FCRA requires credit reporting agencies to use "reasonable procedures" to maintain accurate records—so, there was a clear violation of a statutorily granted right of all 8,000 class members—only those 1,800 who had their credit reports shared could sue because only they had experienced "concrete reputational harm" (having other people tell you are potentially a terrorist when you aren't is defamatory). The other 6,332 individuals may have experienced a statutory violation of their rights, but because their information wasn't shared with anyone outside of TransUnion, they had no "standing"—no right to sue in court—because they didn't

---

[25]   *Id.* at 17, 89–91, 261–63.
[26]   141 S. Ct. 2190, 2205 (2021) (citing *Spokeo, Inc. v. Robins*, 578 U.S. 330, 341 (2016)).
[27]   *Id.* at 2201.
[28]   *Id.* at 2201–02.
[29]   *Id.* at 2202.
[30]   *Id.* at 2208–11.

face any real, identifiable, concrete injury over and above the violation of a statutory right.[31]

What does this mean for individual privacy rights? In short, even if Congress were to give us individual privacy rights of access, correction, deletion, and so forth, flagrantly denying us those rights would not be grounds for a lawsuit. If individuals want to exercise a private right of action, a much-touted addition to privacy laws that is supposed to give them some real teeth,[32] litigants need to identify concrete and particularized harm over and above a company's brazen disregard of our statutory rights.[33] But U.S. courts have been notoriously and consistently unwilling to recognize anything but the most obvious pecuniary harms in privacy cases.[34] Invasions of privacy can cause myriad harms; the leading law and information scholars Daniel Solove and Danielle Keats Citron have identified 15 clusters of harms, included among them are physical, economic, reputational, psychological, autonomy-based, discrimination-based, and relational harms.[35] Courts could recognize those harms, but they just don't.[36] Introducing individual rights of control into a legal system that built a wall around data-extractive conduct and is utterly uninterested in recognizing the gravity of privacy rights is like putting a feather on a weight scale: it won't register.

---

[31]   *Id.* at 2211–12.
[32]   *See* Lauren Henry Scholz, *Privacy Rights of Action in Privacy Law*, 63 Wm. & Mary L. Rev. 1639, 1644–45 (2022) (arguing that private enforcement of privacy regulations can marshal resources not available to the administrative state).
[33]   Transunion, 141 S. Ct. at 2205–06, 2206 n.2.
[34]   *See* Solove and Citron, *Data-Breach Harms*, *supra* note 14, at 747–55 (describing how three common theories of harm advanced by plaintiffs— risk of future injury to plaintiffs, out-of-pocket costs to mitigate the risk of identity theft or fraud, and emotional distress caused by data breaches— have been rejected by courts); Citron and Solove, *Privacy Harms*, *supra* note 14, at 816–19.
[35]   Citron and Solove, *Privacy Harms*, *supra* note 14, at 830.
[36]   *Id.* at 831–61.

5.4   The expressive critique

Law has expressive value.[37] That means that law not only reflects social mores, but also sends messages about what is right and wrong.[38] It sets norms.[39] Privacy laws that elevate individual rights of control send two messages: (1) that privacy is an individual right against others and that privacy is the individual's responsibility and (2) that it is up to us to manage what happens to data extracted from our social behaviors. Both are wrong, misguided, and ill-suited to the threats posed by the information economy.

Privacy scholarship began with individual rights. To Samuel Warren and Louis Brandeis writing in 1890, privacy was a "right 'to be let alone.'"[40] Privacy was "solitude" and a "retreat from the world," particularly from a press that was increasingly intruding into their lives.[41] Almost 100 years later, in 1967, the canonical privacy scholar Alan Westin was still conceptualizing privacy as individuals' right to decide for themselves when, how, and to whom to disclose information.[42]

But in the decades since, privacy scholars have rightly recognized the limitations of the individual model. Privacy is about facilitating social interaction, not stopping it.[43] It is "shorthand for breathing room to engage in the processes of boundary management that enable and constitute self-development. So understood, privacy is fundamentally

---

[37]   See Cass R. Sunstein, *On the Expressive Function of Law*, 144 U. Pa. L. Rev. 2021, 2031 (1996).
[38]   Danielle Keats Citron, *Law's Expressive Value in Combating Cyber Gender Harassment*, 108 Mich. L. Rev. 373, 377 (2009); see also Danielle Keats Citron, *Cyber Civil Rights*, 89 B.U. L. Rev. 61, 90 (2009) (arguing that civil rights prosecutions for cyber harassment would communicate society's commitment to equality).
[39]   See Elizabeth S. Scott, *Social Norms and the Legal Regulation of Marriage*, 86 Va. L. Rev. 1901, 1904–05 (2000) (discussing how the legal framework surrounding marriage prescribed and reinforced social norms).
[40]   Samuel D. Warren and Louis D. Brandeis, *The Right to Privacy*, 4 Harv. L. Rev. 193, 195 (1890).
[41]   *Id.* at 196.
[42]   Alan F. Westin, Privacy and Freedom 7 (1967).
[43]   Danielle Keats Citron, The Fight For Privacy 108 (2022); Ari Ezra Waldman, Privacy As Trust 69-71 (2018).

dynamic."[44] And, importantly, privacy is about power. As Neil Richards notes, "[s]truggles over 'privacy' are in reality struggles over the rules that constrain the power that human information confers."[45] And that power is an important piece of social structure that determines who has access to the "common relationships in contemporary commercial and civic life."[46] Privacy theory, Julie Cohen argues, "should acknowledge that fact."[47]

The law and technology scholar Margot Kaminski argues that because privacy is commonly understood as an individual right against others, grounding privacy law in individual rights makes intuitive sense and would align with individuals' expectations.[48] Even assuming this individualized vision is dominant among nonexperts, that mere fact is no reason to codify those conceptions into law. It is instead a powerful reason for law to push back to frame privacy as a collective goal of democratic governance, especially given the weaknesses of rights, as discussed above. Law can, and should, set stronger norms.

Legislation focused on individual privacy rights of control also sends a message about personal responsibility. Daniel Solove used the phrase "privacy self-management" to describe practices of notice and choice.[49] Individual rights-based laws double down on this model. They put the onus on us to monitor and regulate what happens with extracted data. And we are simply not up to that task at scale. There are simply too many choices, privacy policies, buttons to toggle, and cookies to understand. Plus, even if it were possible for us to manage all that on our own, the information economy is so vast and opaque that individuals will always lack enough information about the downstream effects of data processing to make informed decisions.

Individual responsibility will not solve collective problems. In fact, corporate interests use the discourse of individual responsibility as a shield

---

44   Julie E. Cohen, *What Privacy is For*, 126 HARV. L. REV. 1904, 1906 (2013).
45   NEIL RICHARDS, WHY PRIVACY MATTERS 39 (2022) (emphasis omitted).
46   Julie E. Cohen, *Turning Privacy Inside Out*, 20 THEORETICAL INQUIRIES L. 1, 22 (2019).
47   *Id.*
48   Kaminski, *supra* note 1.
49   Daniel J. Solove, *Introduction: Privacy Self-Management and the Consent Dilemma*, 126 HARV. L. REV. 1880, 1880-82 (2013).

to deflect accountability. We see it all the time, and nowhere more prominently than in the discourse around climate change.

For decades, polluters—such as large oil companies, plastics producers, and the coal industry—have worked to keep the conversation about climate change and its solutions focused on the consumer.[50] As Geoffrey Supran and Naomi Oreskes have found, polluters use the rhetoric of climate "risk" and consumer energy "demand" to downplay the reality and seriousness of climate change, normalize fossil consumption, and individualize responsibility.[51] These communications and marketing strategies have allowed polluters to effectively minimize the appearance of their role in climate change and challenge climate litigation, regulation, and activism.[52] This makes polluters "part of a lineage of industrial producers of harmful commodities that have used personal responsibility framings to disavow themselves."[53]

Here's another example: "The container industry spent tens of millions of dollars to defeat key 'bottle bill' referendums in California and Colorado, and then vigorously advanced recycling—not reuse—as a more practical alternative."[54] The industry did this because recycling "stress[es] the individual's act of disposal" and shifts responsibility away from the producer that inundates the market with plastic in the first place.[55] The push for recycling, therefore, is part of a discourse that gives life to a "diagnosis of environmental ills that places human laziness and ignorance center-stage."[56] The result is predictable inaction on the things that could actually save our planet: "When responsibility for environmental problems is

---

[50]   See, e.g., Geoffrey Supran and Naomi Oreskes, *Rhetoric and Frame Analysis of ExxonMobil's Climate Change Communications*, 4 ONE EARTH 696, 706, 710 (2021) (finding that ExxonMobil disproportionately employed rhetoric to present consumers as responsible for the cause of and treatment for global warming); Walter Lamb, *Keep America Beautiful: Grassroots Non-Profit or Tobacco Front Group?*, 8 PR WATCH 1, 1 (2001) (describing the infamous "crying Indian" ad that expressed the idea that cleaning up the environment was an individual's responsibility, not the tobacco industry's).
[51]   Supran and Oreskes, *supra* note 50, at 706, 708.
[52]   *Id.* at 708, 710–11.
[53]   *Id.* at 712.
[54]   Michael F. Maniates, *Individualization: Plant a Tree, Buy a Bike, Save the World?*, 1 GLOB. ENV'T POL. 31, 43 (2001) (emphasis omitted).
[55]   Id.
[56]   *Id.*

individualized, there is little room to ponder institutions, the nature and exercise of political power, or ways of collectively changing the distribution of power and influence in society—to, in other words, 'think institutionally.'"[57] This is why the plastics industry has waged a decades-long, multimillion-dollar campaign to perpetuate the myth of plastic recyclability and to push recycling—a decidedly individual-focused effort—as the ultimate solution to our impending climate catastrophe.[58]

The information industry is taking its cues from big polluters. Technology companies publish statements about transparency,[59] but fire researchers as soon as their scholarship highlights biases and erasure encoded in profitable algorithms.[60] Industry mouthpieces will focus on consent and access when any issue comes up,[61] but never speak about industry's power to control the collection and processing of data without any accountability from independent researchers.[62] The industry will spend millions of dollars focusing on making data use policies more readable, but then begin to design an entire virtual world that is data extractive at its core.[63] Information companies protect their bottom line by utilizing these sleight of hand tactics to distract the public with empty gestures while continuing to collect and sell their private data.

That said, is individual responsibility really that bad? Following the climate analogy, it makes sense for us to reduce our carbon footprints

---

[57]   *Id.* at 33.

[58]   *Frontline: Plastic Wars* (PBS television broadcast Mar. 31, 2020), https:// www.pbs.org/wgbh/frontline/documentary/plastic-wars/.

[59]   ARI EZRA WALDMAN, INDUSTRY UNBOUND: THE INSIDE STORY OF PRIVACY, DATA, AND CORPORATE POWER 67–68 (2021).

[60]   See, e.g., Cade Metz and Daisuke Wakabayashi, Google Researcher Says She Was Fired Over Paper Highlighting Bias in A.I., N.Y. TIMES (Dec. 3, 2020), https://www.nytimes.com/2020/12/03/technology/google-researcher -timnit-gebru.html.

[61]   WALDMAN, *supra* note 59, at 67–70.

[62]   *See, e.g.*, Taylor Hatmaker, *Facebook Cuts off NYU Researcher Access, Prompting Rebuke from Lawmakers*, TECHCRUNCH (Aug. 4, 2021, 2:17 PM), https://techcrunch.com/2021/08/04/facebook-ad-observatory-nyu -researchers/.

[63]   *See, e.g.*, Kate O'Flaherty, *Why Facebook's Metaverse Is a Privacy Nightmare*, FORBES (Nov. 13, 2021, 6:30 AM), https://www.forbes.com/ sites/kateoflahertyuk/2021/11/13/why-facebooks-metaverse-is-a-privacy -nightmare/?sh=638254fc6db8 .

even if other regulatory responses could have more impact. It's something, and something is better than nothing. But is it? As the next section suggests, individual rights often crowd out other regulatory options. By sending a message of individual responsibility, the information industry ensures that collective, corporate responsibility dies.

5.5   The structural critique

Individual rights are classic liberal responses to social problems.[64] But individual rights, as described by critical legal theorists, can be indeterminate: "[N]othing whatever follows from a court's adoption of some" new legal right for individuals.[65] They can also be pyrrhic victories: "[W]inning a legal victory [recognizing an individual right] can actually impede further progressive change."[66] This is precisely what is happening with individual privacy rights of control.

Paul Butler illustrates the "critique of rights" in the context of the right to counsel for indigent defendants. Butler argues that *Gideon v. Wainwright*,[67] long regarded as a milestone in criminal justice because it guaranteed poor criminal defendants the right to be represented by an attorney, "obscures" the real problems of the criminal justice system.[68] The reason "prisons are filled with poor people, and that rich people rarely go to prison" is not that the former have no lawyers and the latter have all the good ones; rather, it is "because prison is for the poor, and not

---

[64]   See JAMES E. FLEMING AND LINDA C. McCLAIN, ORDERED LIBERTY 1–4 (2013).

[65]   Mark Tushnet, *The Critique of Rights*, 47 SMU L. REV. 23, 32 (1993). That said, many scholars have been more charitable about rights, recognizing their discursive and organizing potential. *See, e.g.*, Patricia J. Williams, *Alchemical Notes: Reconstructing Ideals from Deconstructed Rights*, 22 HARV. C.R.-C.L. L. REV. 401, 410 (1987) ("[R]ights rhetoric has been and continues to be an effective form of discourse for blacks.").

[66]   Tushnet, *supra* note 65, at 26; *see* Alan David Freeman, *Legitimizing Racial Discrimination Through Antidiscrimination Law: A Critical Review of Supreme Court Doctrine*, 62 MINN. L. REV. 1049, 1051–52 (1978) (referring to the legitimizing capacities of legal doctrine).

[67]   372 U.S. 335 (1963).

[68]   Paul D. Butler, *Poor People Lose: Gideon and the Critique of Rights*, 122 YALE L.J. 2176, 2178 (2013).

the rich."[69] Butler recognizes that *Gideon* itself did not create a carceral state that imprisons poor people of color at rates far higher than any other group.[70] Instead, Butler argues that by providing indigent defendants with counsel—that perfect patina of procedural due process, especially from the lawyer's perspective—*Gideon* legitimized a broken, racist system and diffused political resistance to structural change.[71] *Gideon* did not ensure that poor Black people would be "stopped less, arrested less, prosecuted less, incarcerated less."[72] It gave defendants a fairer process, but also made it harder for social movements to argue that the system was broken. In other words, *Gideon* threw an individual right at a structural problem, promised us that rights would make the structural problem less of a problem, and, ultimately, made the problem worse.[73] The carceral state grew, and it grew even more skewed against people of color.[74] But it maintained legitimacy because *Gideon* gave defendants equal process.

By focusing on each individual defendant's right to counsel, *Gideon* cut off collective action. As Wendy Brown noted, rights discourse "convert[ed] social problems into matters of individualized, dehistoricized injury and entitlement."[75] It diverted scholarly and policymaker attention to the boundaries of the right and away from the pressing need to find actual answers to the problems of mass incarceration of poor people of color.

The discourse of individual responsibility did the same thing in the climate change context. Studies show that merely reminding individuals of their own past efforts and actions to reduce energy consumption decreases support for government action on climate change.[76] Individual

---

69   *Id.*
70   Id.
71   *Id.* at 2178–79.
72   *Id.* at 2191.
73   *Id.* at 2178–79. The rights-only liberal response worked alongside other aspects of the criminal justice system, like the imposition of strict sentencing guidelines that sentenced those convicted of possession of small amounts of drugs to decades in prison, to worsen the problems of the carceral state. *See, e.g.*, Jessica M. Eaglin, *The Perils of "Old" and "New" in Sentencing Reform*, 76 N.Y.U. ANN. SURV. AM. L. 355, 365 (2021).
74   *See* Butler, *supra* note 68, at 2178.
75   WENDY BROWN, STATES OF INJURY 124 (1995).
76   Seth H. Werfel, *Household Behaviour Crowds Out Support for Climate Change Policy When Sufficient Progress Is Perceived*, 7 NATURE CLIMATE CHANGE 512, 512 (2017).

household behavior crowds out public support for government action by creating the perception of sufficient progress.[77]

In the privacy space, individual rights look good on paper. Legislators will throw some rights at a political and economic problem, point to the bill they passed, and say, "Look what we did!" When, inevitably, the data-extractive economy makes headlines for its privacy invasions, manipulative tactics, and violations of civil rights—none of which are limited by individual rights—conservative and neoliberal policymakers will claim that too much regulation stifles innovation, insist they addressed the problem, and go home.[78] Individual rights leave extractive business models wholly intact. As a result, privacy social movements—already hamstrung by the mostly invisible nature of information age harms—and privacy civil society—heavily invested in their seats at the table—will be less able to galvanize interest in structural reform. If we start with individual rights, we will likely end with them, too.

5.6 Conclusion

By now it should be clear that the second wave's rights model is a gift to industry. Individuals can exercise their rights to delete their data and to transfer it if they wish, but policymakers' focus on individual responsibility entirely ignores those who are primarily responsible for the manipulation, subordination, and commodification at the heart of informational capitalism. Nor is it enough to say that individual rights should be one piece in a larger regulatory regime. When legislators begin with individual responsibility, they rarely, if ever, follow through with the kind of structural regulation that could make individual rights meaningful. Therefore, the individual rights model is a trap, laid for us by corporate actors and captured lawmakers content with symbolic performances of regulation.

But the second wave is not only about rights. Companies that collect and use data about individuals also have to engage in procedural compliance. These "rules of the game" are meant to keep privacy in mind during corporate daily life. They don't. As the next chapter shows, the compliance

---

[77]   *Id.* at 513.
[78]   *See* COHEN, *supra* note 24, at 89–91.

side of the second wave's rights-compliance model is another opportunity for data extractive corporations to legitimize their predatory behavior without actually limiting much of it.

6 Symbolic compliance and the managerialization of privacy law

In the last chapter, we discussed the limitations of individual privacy rights of control. However, as we discussed in Chapter 4, individual rights are just one half of the second wave of U.S. privacy law. The other half relies on internal structures of compliance. The compliance side of rights/ compliance model in the second wave are mostly procedural structures— new privacy offices and staffs, impact assessments, record keeping, and the like—that are supposed to keep privacy at the forefront of everything technology companies do, from design to sales and marketing, and to provide some form of paper trail for privacy work. Compliance is also big business these days. There are compliance departments at most major companies (not just about privacy), thousands of compliance professionals hired each year, and hundreds of privacy compliance vendors eager to sell their services to any company that collects consumer data. But compliance is not just a practice. Its inclusion in second wave privacy law also represents a normative commitment to a form of collaborative governance that relies on regulated entities monitoring themselves. That means that the compliance side of the rights/compliance model is uniquely subject to capture.

But the problems of the compliance model run deeper. This chapter focuses on five of them. First, a framing critique demonstrates how the compliance model, by permitting the goal of privacy law to be recast as minimizing risk to the companies rather minimizing privacy risks to consumers, falls to the underlying, pro-corporate logics of risk management. Second, the symbolic critique shows how procedural compliance is easily (and often) reduced to box-checking, making paperwork a meaningless end in itself. Third, a power critique highlights the importance of what procedural compliance misses—namely, the distributive injustices of data-extractive capitalism that affect marginalized communities the most. Fourth, the competition critique suggests that because many of the practices incorporated into second-wave privacy law were endogenously created, from the ground-up, by the largest and wealthiest technology companies, their entrenchment in law conscripts the second wave into supporting the anticompetitive behavior of the information industry's largest actors. Fifth and finally, an internal critique shows how the practical application of compliance-based governance is internally inconsistent, creating public institutions that are incapable of holding industry accountable. Like the previous chapter, this chapter treats each critique in turn.

6.1   The framing critique

Relying on internal compliance structures for privacy law means that the structures companies create—and the managers who design them—become the loci at which privacy law is negotiated, addressed, and implemented on a regular basis. This opens a window for managerial and other industry-friendly discourses and practices to frame what the law looks like on the ground, or as it's implemented in real life. In other words, it almost doesn't matter what legislators put in their laws. As long as they give interpretive and implementing power to industry in a public-private partnership, the law is going to operate the way industry wants. In the second wave, laws designed to require companies to assess privacy risks to consumers are recast in this liminal space to focus on the litigation risks of companies. As a result, second-wave privacy law falls prey to the anti-regulatory logics of cost-benefit analysis. This is the framing critique.

The sociolegal scholar Lauren Edelman highlighted a similar phenomenon in antidiscrimination law. In her book, *Working Law*, Edelman showed how form over substance in corporate compliance with civil rights law was having a deleterious effect on real progress toward workplace equality. She found that despite Title VII of the Civil Rights Act's substantive prohibition on sex discrimination, companies were responding not with equal treatment for all genders, but with in-house structures of compliance. These trainings, anti-discrimination policies, complaint procedures, and diversity offices, just to name a few, were then weaponized to demonstrate compliance with Title VII even though gender equity had not improved on the ground. Federal courts in the U.S. were all too willing to endorse these symbols of compliance as what the law actually required, a phenomenon Edelman called "legal endogeneity" because the law was defined from within, from the evasive practices of the very organizations the law was supposed to regulate.[1]

The first step in the legal endogeneity spiral happens when corporate actors are given the power to determine what the law means in practice. As Edelman describes, these professionals "make certain laws or norms visible or invisible to employers and frame those laws' relevance to organizational life." In so doing, they shape the "aesthetic of the law," determining not just what laws make it through the filter, but what those legal obligations look like.[2] Human resources professionals and lawyers figure prominently in Edelman's work on the implementation (or lack thereof) of civil rights laws; they frame the work compliance with Title VII as minimizing the risk of a lawsuit from an employee, rather than actually eradicating sex discrimination in the workplace. In the privacy space, lawyers, chief privacy officers, consultants, and their staffs assume the principal legal filter role and should ideally frame corporate legal obligations in terms of the laws' underlying purposes—namely, to create more robust privacy protections, to protect consumers from predatory data collection practices, and to minimize privacy risks to consumers.

But that is not always what happens. In-house counsel routinely use their legal expertise to advance their employers' financial interests, allowing their companies to make more money, pay fewer taxes, escape liability, and reach new markets. Lawyers also needed to maintain their seat at the table by "mak[ing] their advice more palatable to businesspeople."[3] As a result, many privacy lawyers and privacy professionals frame privacy law compliance as a means of minimizing the risk to the company, not protecting consumers from data use harms.

This risk framing pervades the privacy compliance landscape. The National Institute of Standards and Technology (NIST), which has sig-

---

[1]   LAUREN EDELMAN, WORKING LAW (2016).
[2]   Id. at 82.
[3]   Robert L. Nelson and Laura Beth Nielsen, *Cops, Counsel, and Entrepreneurs: Constructing the Role of Inside Counsel in Large Corporations*, 34 LAW & SOC'Y REV. 457, 474-77 (2000).

nificant influence on how the government and businesses think about privacy and security, explicitly frames corporate privacy obligations as "the management of organizational risk."[4] Law firms run risk minimization Continuing Legal Education programs that focus entirely on risks to the company.[5] Privacy trade groups also frame compliance as a means of minimizing corporate risk. For example, the International Association of Privacy Professionals (IAPP), a trade organization for privacy professionals, and TrustArc, a leading privacy compliance vendor, published a study focusing on prioritizing different parts of GDPR based on the risks of noncompliance to the company.[6] And the organization has also framed data minimization as a way of reducing corporate risk and hosted several webinars in which experts have said that the "heart" of data protection compliance is doing what "you can to manage the risk to the company" posed by new privacy laws.[7] This focus ultimately encourages many companies to house their privacy officers within their risk management departments,[8] but it also puts a decidedly corporate spin on privacy law itself.

Framing the data privacy landscape as one based on corporate risk is not surprising. Risk framing can actually encourage compliance with the law by persuading executives to treat it as a high priority,[9] especially since some executives still see privacy as inconsistent with corporate profit goals. The risk of a fine of four percent of global revenue goes a long way to making privacy compliance a central corporate mission.[10] Risk

---

4   *Risk Management*, NAT'L INST. OF STANDARDS AND TECH., https://csrc.nist .gov/Projects/Risk-Management/rmf-overview.

5   *See, e.g., Privacy and Data Protection: Managing Your Litigation Risk*, PERKINS COIE.

6   IAPP & TRUSTARC, GETTING TO GDPR COMPLIANCE: RISK EVALUATION AND STRATEGIES FOR MITIGATION (2018), https://iapp.org/news/a/event -privacy-and-data-protection-managing-your-litigation-risk/.

7   *Reducing Risk Through Data Minimization*, IAPP (Sept. 6, 2016), https:// iapp.org/store/webconferences/a0l1a000002hDCIAA2/; *The Role of Risk Management in Data Protection*, IAPP (Jan. 23, 2015), https://iapp.org/ store/webconferences/a0l1a000000SKCzAAO/.

8   Kenneth A. Bamberger and Deirdre K. Mulligan, New Governance, Chief Privacy Officers, and the Corporate Management of Information Privacy in the United States: An Initial Inquiry, 33 LAW & POL'Y 477, 488, 493–94 (2011).

9   *See* EDELMAN, *supra* note 1, at 98.

10 General Data Protection Regulation, arts. 58, 83, at 70, 82.

framing also makes sense from an endogenous political perspective. By emphasizing the dangers of noncompliance, privacy professionals stake out important territory at the highest levels of corporate decision-making, giving them seats at the table and the capacity to influence policy. And third-party vendors follow suit because it allows them to increase their market share and emphasize the importance of their services.[11]

But risk framing is problematic if the goal is adherence to the substantive goals of privacy law. Risk framing is not only too narrow, but also a trick, a misdirection with significant normative implications. Focusing on the avoidance of a *corporate* problem rather than the achievement of an affirmative *social* goal—namely, greater user control, privacy, and safety—orients privacy law toward corporate welfare (not coincidentally, a central facet of neoliberalism).

Importantly, doing privacy within a risk management frame also reduces privacy to things that can be quantified: a cost here, revenue there. This logic of quantification of privacy law leaves out all the things that cannot be appreciated on a corporate balance sheet. Privacy also involves managing users' expectations, their desire for obscurity, their need for trust, and their consistent distaste for transfers of data to third parties. Plus, risk management gives corporate actors the power and responsibility to decide the value of privacy; in other words, it is the very people with a strong interest in data extraction who get to decide how much a privacy risk is worth. The second wave's reliance on internal structures of compliance puts the power of framing privacy into the hands of people with a keen interest on seeing privacy risks as rare and insignificant.

6.2   The symbolic critique

Having given corporations the power to interpret privacy law in corporate-friendly terms like the management of corporate risk rather than in terms of substantive privacy protections for users, compliance professionals then have the chance to create structures, services, and technologies to comply with their version of the law. Some of these structures are reflected in specific provisions of a statute. For example, because the

---

[11]   *See* EDELMAN, *supra* note 1, at 97-8.

FTC often requires regulated companies to implement a "comprehensive privacy program" and because the GDPR requires the designation of a data protection officer (DPO), many companies have to hire a DPO.[12] Similarly, because the GDPR gives consumers a right to access their information and a right to erase irrelevant, incorrect, and outdated information,[13] data collectors have to develop systems to find and categorize user data. But where legal requirements are flexible—What is a CPO/DPO supposed to do? How do companies have to present their data use practices to users? How are companies supposed to design products with privacy in mind?—compliance structures often become merely symbolic.

Symbolic structures are those that carry with them an instant perception of legitimacy because they resemble pre-existing forms already having the imprimatur of the law. A nondiscrimination policy, with legal-sounding terms of art, or internal dispute resolution systems are examples of symbolic structures that resemble legal processes.[14] But when these structures become merely symbolic, when they offer just the veneer or the trappings of compliance with no substance, then they can frustrate the goals of the law. This is what is happening in privacy law's second wave.

Over the last 20 years, many companies have developed increasingly complex privacy structures, hired CPOs and downstream privacy professionals, and created protocols to manage access to personal data, among many other steps.[15] But many of these structures have become merely symbolic because they have been reduced to flow charts, check lists, and templates.[16] Third-party technology vendors provide checklists and templates, as well. For example, Nymity offers an automated "privacy

---

12   *See* GDPR, Arts 37–39; Agreement Containing Consent Order at 4, *In re Google, Inc.*, Docket No. C-4336, No. 102 3136 (F.T.C. Oct. 24, 2011) [hereinafter Google Consent Decree], https://www.ftc.gov/sites/default/files/documents/cases/2011/10/111024googlebuzzdo.pdf.

13   GDPR, Arts 15, 17, 43–44.

14   *See* EDELMAN, *supra* note 1, at 101.

15   KENNETH BAMBERGER AND DEIRDRE MULLIGAN, PRIVACY ON THE GROUND 83-86 (2015).

16   Ari Ezra Waldman, *Privacy Law's False Promise*, 97 WASH. U. L. REV. 773, 803-07 (2020).

program ... made up of policies, procedures, and other accountability mechanisms."[17] Data collectors snap up these tools with alacrity.

A central element of second-wave privacy governance is the audit, but it too has become merely symbolic. The FTC requires companies operating under consent decrees to submit assessments roughly every two years for the life of the order.[18] Assessments have to be completed by a "qualified, objective, independent third-party" auditor with sufficient experience. And they must describe specific privacy controls, evaluate their adequacy given the size and scope of the company, explain how they meet FTC requirements, and certify they are operating effectively.[19] They have been heralded as game changers.[20]

In reality, assessments have failed to achieve that goal because some of them have become mere symbols of compliance. The FTC requires assessments, and assessments are not the intense, independent, under-the-hood investigations we think of when we think of audits. They leave wiggle room for regulated companies. Audits are independent third-party analyses, where the auditors themselves review evidence and make conclusions independent of the audit subject. Assessments are based on assertions from management rather than wholly independent analyses from auditors, and are usually framed by goals set by management.[21] That means

---

[17]   Nymity, 2018 Privacy Compliance Software Buyer's Guide 9 (2018), https://info.nymity.com/hubfs/2018%20Privacy%20Compliance%20Software%20Buyers%20Guide/Nymity-Buyers-Guide-GDPR-Edition.pdf.

[18]   See, e.g., In re Google, Inc., FTC File No. 102 3136, No. C-4336 (Oct. 13, 2011) [hereinafter Google Order], https://www.ftc.gov/sites/default/files/documents/cases/2011/10/111024googlebuzzdo.pdf; Decision and Order at 4, FTC File No. 092 3093, No. C-4316 (Mar. 2, 2011), https://www.ftc.gov/sites/default/files/documents/cases/2011/03/110311twitterdo.pdf.

[19]   Google Order, supra note 18, at 5.

[20]   Jessica Leber, The FTC's Privacy Cop Cracks Down, MIT Tech. Rev. (June 26, 2012), https://www.technologyreview.com/s/428342/the-ftcs-privacy-cop-cracks-down/; Kashmir Hill, So What Are These Privacy Audits That Google and Facebook Have To Do For the Next 20 Years?, Forbes (Nov. 31. 2011), https://www.forbes.com/sites/kashmirhill/2011/11/30/so-what-are-these-privacy-auditsthat-google-and-facebook-have-to-do-for-the-next-20-years/.

[21]   Megan Gray, Understanding and Improving Privacy "Audits" Under FTC Orders, Stan. L. Sch. Center for Internet & Soc. 6 (Apr. 18, 2018), https://cyberlaw.stanford.edu/files/blogs/white%20paper%204.18.18.pdf.

that the company that is supposed to be the subject of the assessment is, in fact, determining the bases upon which it gets evaluated, thus giving companies some power to predetermine the results. For example, the FTC wanted an assessment to ensure that Google had a privacy team, an ongoing and flexible privacy assessment process, relationships with vendors capable of protecting data, and a few other related requirements.[22] But based on a redacted version of the report, the assessment used conclusory language that was based almost entirely on Google proffers. The report states that "Google has implemented a privacy risk assessment process in order to identify reasonably foreseeable, material risks, both internal and external," tracking the language of the FTC order explicitly.[23] As evidence for this conclusory statement, the report refers the reader to Google's responses to the auditor's questions, not any actual evidence.[24] Later, the report concludes that "Google's privacy controls were operating with sufficient effectiveness to provide reasonable assurance to protect the privacy of covered information ... " based only on "the Google Privacy Program set forth in Attachment A of Management's Assertion in Exhibit I."[25] In other words, the only evidence showing that Google met FTC requirements was Google's statements to that effect. The fact that these assessments can be fulfilled through rough conclusory statements without independent investigation shows how assessments can become mere symbols of compliance.

As we discussed in the last chapter, it is already difficult to vindicate privacy rights. By focusing on compliance paper trails and symbols of compliance, the managerialization of privacy law makes vindicating privacy rights even harder. When a company can claim that it should not be held responsible for data misuse because, despite privacy problems in a final product, they completed a private impact assessment and documented internal approaches to privacy issues and completed an assessment, individuals and regulators are both immediately put on the defensive and may be dissuaded from mobilizing their rights and

---

22   Google Consent Decree, *supra* note 18, at 5–6.
23   FED. TRADE COMM'N, INITIAL ASSESSMENT REPORT ON GOOGLE'S PRIVACY PROGRAM FOR THE PERIOD OCT. 29, 2011 – APR. 25, 2012, at 9 (Sept. 25 2012), https://epic.org/privacy/ftc/googlebuzz/FTC-Initial-Assessment-09–26–12.pdf.
24   *Id.*
25   *Id.* at 14.

investigative powers in the first place.[26] Granted, the GDPR includes documentation requirements; companies need reports to prove they took "reasonable and appropriate" steps to protect consumer privacy under FTC consent decrees. But the way some market players conflate the structure of compliance (the records) with actual compliance (following the GDPR) is striking.

6.3   The power critique

As we have seen, the enforcement toolkit in recent U.S. privacy proposals is largely procedural: impact assessments, privacy officers, and internal policies. That means that laws will rely on internal organizational structures to protect the individual rights guaranteed on the face of the laws. The focus on documentation as an end in itself elevates a merely symbolic structure to evidence of actual compliance with the law, obscuring the underlying structural inequities left intact. As a structural matter, the second wave's approach to data governance elides the asymmetries of power that define informational capitalism.[27] This is the critique of power—namely, that the second wave is agnostic as to the power relations of informational capitalism.

Rules that put procedural requirements around the status quo do not change it. And that status quo is one of extraordinary power imbalance, with power concentrated in the hands of a few powerful companies. Through data extraction and processing, the information industry has the power to influence much our existence—what we read, think, see, want, and even understand to be true can be manipulated by weaponized data-driven tools.[28] Technology companies conscript us in the commodification and subordination of others.[29] Their products discriminate, subordinate, and undermine democracy.[30] Requiring a company to complete

---

[26]   *See* Julie E. Cohen, Between Truth and Power: Legal Constructions of Informational Capitalism 145 (2019).

[27]   Julie E. Cohen, *What Privacy Is For*, 126 Harv. L. Rev. 1904, 1905 (2013).

[28]   *Id.* at 1916–17 (describing the "modulated society").

[29]   Salomé Viljoen, *A Relational Theory of Data Governance*, 131 Yale L.J. 573 (2021).

[30]   *E.g.*, Siva Vaidhyanathan, Anti-Social Media: How Facebook Disconnects Us and Undermines Democracy (2018); Solon Barocas

an impact assessment before processing data not only leaves those power structures intact, but also suggests that redistributing that power simply isn't the second wave's goal.

Even worse, procedural guardrails that amount to little more than symbols may actually legitimize informational capitalism's power relations, entrenching them rather than just leaving them in place. Legitimizing procedures disaggregate legitimacy from substantive justice. Procedures offer "no framework for thinking systematically about the interrelationships between political and economic power."[31] They substitute the "political judgment" of traditional regulation and government intervention with "technical management" of the market, thereby leaving unanswered and unresolved vexing questions of inequality, subordination, manipulation, and asymmetrical power.[32] After all, data can be a tool of oppression, whether it is exploited to train totalitarian facial recognition models, surveil protestors, send people to jail, or subjugate vulnerable populations.[33] For those people society pushes to the margins, privacy is particularly important and data-extraction particularly dangerous. Disclosures, data breaches, and industry negligence with pornography sites, WiFi-enabled sex toys, and femtech products undermine a core human right of sexual privacy for everyone, but the people who are most hurt are the most marginalized in society.[34] Compliance practices do little to ameliorate or stop these harms other than to encourage companies to

---

and Andrew D. Selbst, *Big Data's Disparate Impact*, 104 CALIF. L. REV. 671, 694-714 (2016); Danielle Keats Citron and Frank Pasquale, *The Scored Society: Due Process for Automated Predictions*, 89 WASH. L. REV. 1, 27-32 (2014); Sonia K. Katyal, *Private Accountability in the Age of Artificial Intelligence*, 66 U.C.L.A. L. REV. 54, 70-77 (2019); Julia Angwin, Jeff Larson, Surya Mattu and Lauren Kirchner, *Machine Bias*, PROPUBLICA (May 23, 2016), https://www.propublica.org/article/machine-bias-risk-assessments -in-criminal-sentencing.

[31]   Jedediah Britton-Purdy, David Singh Grewal, Amy Kapczynski and K. Sabeel Rahman, *Building a Law-and-Political-Economy Framework: Beyond the Twentieth-Century Synthesis*, 129 YALE L.J. 1796, 1790 (2020).

[32]   *Id.* at 1793.

[33]   *E.g.*, SAFIYA NOBLE, ALGORITHMS OF OPPRESSION: HOW SEARCH ENGINES REINFORCE RACISM (2018); RUHA BENJAMIN, RACE AFTER TECHNOLOGY (2019); Rashida Richardson, Jason Shultz, and Kate Crawford, *Dirty Data, Bad Predictions: How Civil Rights Violations Impact Police Data, Predictive Policing Systems, and Justice*, 94 N.Y.U. L. REV. 192 (2019).

[34]   Danielle Keats Citron, *A New Compact for Sexual Privacy*, 62 WILLIAM & MARY L. REV. 1763, 1770 (2021).

put things down on paper. There are, however, some practices that no amount of procedural due process can fix.

That is a fatal blind spot. The second wave conceptualizes privacy as personal control over data and tries to achieve that goal by laying down "rules of the road" for data use rather than restructuring a data-extractive business model to rein in information industry power.[35] But informational capitalism creates population-level harms, not merely atomistic ones. It puts marginalized populations at unique risks.[36] It normalizes surveillance and attendant behavior manipulation. Critical privacy scholars recognize this; the second wave does not. Scholars and policymakers should continue to interrogate the conceptions of privacy underlying new approaches to privacy law. As they do, they may find that privacy law has been a sham from the beginning.

6.4   The competition critique

The second wave did not just emerge out of nowhere. As we discussed in Chapter 4, the rights/compliance model of the second wave predated the GDPR and the CCPA. Rather than learning from these pieces of legislation, the second wave emerged endogenously from the practices that industry has been developing internally all along.[37] There are many problems with this, not the least of which is that following the practices of industry tends to privilege the practices of industry's biggest players,

---

[35]   Meg Leta Jones and Margot E. Kaminski, *An American's Guide to the GDPR*, 98 DENV. L. REV. 93, 108, 110 (2020) (explaining that the GDPR is a compliance regime that outlines how personal data can be processed lawfully).

[36]   *See e.g.,* DANIELLE KEATS CITRON, THE FIGHT FOR PRIVACY (2022); ANITA L. ALLEN, UNEASY ACCESS: PRIVACY FOR WOMEN IN A FREE SOCIETY (1988); SCOTT SKINNER-THOMPSON, PRIVACY AT THE MARGINS 2 (2021); Anita L. Allen, *Gender and Privacy in Cyberspace*, 52 Stan. L. Rev. 1175, 1178 (2000); Anita L. Allen, *Privacy Torts: Unreliable Remedies for LGBT Plaintiffs*, 98 Calif. L. Rev. 1711, 1721 (2010); Danielle Keats Citron, *Cyber Civil Rights*, 89 B.U. L. Rev. 61, 70, 85 (2009); Danielle Keats Citron and Mary Anne Franks, *Criminalizing Revenge Porn*, 49 Wake Forest L. Rev. 345, 347-48 (2014); Danielle Keats Citron, *Sexual Privacy*, 128 Yale L.J. 1870, 1908 (2019).

[37]   Ari Ezra Waldman, *Privacy, Practice, and Performance*, 110 CAL. L. REV. 1221, 1233-251 (2022).

conscripting the law in entrenched parties' anti-competitive crusades. This is the competition critique.

The endogeneity of privacy law practices means that the law may be constructed by the repeated practices of the most dominant actors—namely, those with money, power, and the risk tolerance that comes with both. There are several reasons for this. These companies' wealth, status, and market share allow them to take on greater litigation risks than their smaller competitors.[38] As such, dominant companies can afford to act first and establish new compliance practices without clear guidance from regulators, just as envisioned by compliance-based governance. And perhaps because smaller competitors cannot afford the risks of investigation and litigation that come with improper compliance practices, industry standards and customs will coalesce around the performances of dominant players.[39]

This coalescing behind the practices of the most dominant actors also happens organically. In many industries, professionals share their experiences and advice through formal outlets—namely, industry conferences, convenings, and publications, where the views of industry leaders are usually of keen interest to the rank-and-file. The privacy industry has several large networking conferences, including several hosted by International Association of Privacy Professionals, attracting thousands of attendees worldwide, and the Privacy+Security Forum, which happens twice a year and brings together hundreds of professionals for panels, networking, and idea exchange. Researchers have also shown that privacy professionals take advantage of their overlapping social networks to learn from colleagues at leading companies.[40] This effectively spreads the com-

---

[38]   George B. Shepherd and Morgan Cloud, *Time and Money: Discovery Leads to Hourly Billing*, 1999 U. ILL. L. REV. 91, 103-04 (1999).

[39]   *See, e.g.*, Eric A. Posner, *Law, Economics, and Inefficient Norms*, 144 U. PA. L. REV. 1697, 1727 (1996) ("highly unequal endowments of group members may be evidence of inefficient norms. The more powerful members may prefer and enforce norms that redistribute wealth to them, even when those norms are inefficient."); Lloyd L. Weinreb, *Custom, Law and Public Policy: The INS Case as an Example for Intellectual Property*, 78 VA. L. REV. 141, 146-47 (1992) (arguing that relying on custom will mean that "the better financed private interest" will win, "rather than a careful, systematic" rule that "will serve the community as a whole.").

[40]   BAMBERGER AND MULLIGAN, *supra* note 15, at 80, 142.

pliance performances of a small subset of industry actors across the field, reinforcing privacy law "isomorphism."[41] Therefore, the most powerful corporations are able to entrench their compliance practices in the same way a first entrant can claim a monopolistic position in a market.

Wealthier companies also have the resources to build larger in-house privacy departments that can dedicate time, money, and labor to compliance practices. Indeed, as the IAPP and TrustArc recently found, budgetary constraints likely explain why many companies have not hired anyone to help with data mapping, data inventories, or privacy impact assessments, despite GDPR requirements.[42] By contrast, smaller companies are forced to outsource more of their compliance to privacy technology vendors, many of which make dubious claims about proprietary automated systems that purport to achieve compliance with pre-filled documents and paper trails.[43] Therefore, a long list of performative compliance practices almost exclusively come from the internal processes of companies that can afford to develop them.

Dominant companies also have more influence over regulators and regulations. In addition to their multi-billion-dollar direct lobbying campaigns aimed at weakening privacy law, the wealthiest technology companies have funded several trade organizations to research and publish policy white papers that reflect their interests.[44] Plus, representatives from the most powerful technology companies have been the most common

---

[41]   *See* Paul DiMaggio and Walter Powell, *The Iron Cage Revisited: Institutional Isomorphism and Collective Rationality in Organizational Fields*, 48 AM. SOCIOLOGICAL REV. 147 (1983) (explaining how and why businesses in an industry evolve to look and behave in similar ways); Mark S. Granovetter, *The Strength of Weak Ties*, 78 AM. J. SOC. 1360, 1363-66 (1973) (discussing how information is spread through the connections that link individuals within their networks and to other networks).

[42]   IAPP & TRUSTARC, GETTING TO GDPR COMPLIANCE: RISK EVALUATION AND STRATEGIES FOR MITIGATION 8-10 (2018), https://iapp.org/media/pdf/resource_center/GDPR-Risks-and-Strategies-FINAL.pdf.

[43]   Ari Ezra Waldman, *Outsourcing Privacy*, 96 NOTRE DAME L. REV. REFLECTION 194 (2021).

[44]   David Dayan, *An Advocacy Group for Startups is Funded by Google and Run by Ex-Googlers*, INTERCEPT (May 30, 2018), https://theintercept.com/2018/05/30/google-engine-advocacy-tech-startups/.

invitees at congressional hearings on privacy.[45] And, given the revolving door between government service and lucrative positions representing technology companies, regulators have a serious incentive to develop stronger relationships with companies like Facebook and Google than with their far smaller competitors.

This is more than a theoretical possibility, and, in fact, is precisely how many interactions play out between regulators and industry. The FTC routinely cites the views of the information industry's largest players in its staff reports. For example, the FTC relied on statements from Google's Director of Public Policy when it emphasized transparency and control in its mobile privacy guidance.[46] The report followed from the advice of the Retail Industry Leaders Association and an industry trade organization funded by wealthy software development interests that calls for "limited government involvement in technology."[47] The FTC also explicitly endorsed Facebook's, Apple's, and Google's use of icons to communicate privacy information.[48] It adopted industry's recommendation for self-regulation and an opt-in "Do Not Track" mechanism.[49] And regulators sided with leading technology companies to support self-regulation of the Internet of Things.[50] It stands to reason that these powerful interests will also have an advantage when they seek to certify their compliance practices and have their versions of best practices adopted as the industry standard.

---

[45]   *E.g.*, *Examining Safeguards for Consumer Data Privacy*, Hearing before the S. Comm. on Commerce, Sci., & Transp., 115th Cong. 2nd sess. (2018) (including testimony from Keith Enright, Google's Chief Privacy Office at the time, and Damien Kieran, Global Data Protection Officer and Associate General Counsel at Twitter, Inc.).

[46]   Fed. Trade Comm'n, Mobile Privacy Disclosures: Building Trust Through Transparency 3 n.13 (2013), https://www.ftc.gov/sites/default/files/documents/reports/mobile-privacy-disclosures-building-trust-through-transparency-federal-trade-commission-staff-report/130201mobileprivacyreport.pdf.

[47]   *Id.* at 13 n. 62.

[48]   *Id.* at 17 & n. 81.

[49]   *Id.* at 21 & n. 92.

[50]   Fed. Trade Comm'n, Internet of Things: Privacy & Security in a Connected World 48-49 (2015), https://www.ftc.gov/system/files/documents/reports/federal-trade-commission-staff-report-november-2013-workshop-entitled-internet-things-privacy/150127iotrpt.pdf.

Therefore, wealthy corporations' performances are more likely to construct the compliance landscape. But what is good for a monopolist is not usually good for society. Entrenched powers have an interest in cementing their market positions, and many have used law to do so.

6.5   The internal critique

The second wave is in a death spiral of its own making. It is internally inconsistent. It fails to create the kind of public institutions necessary to prevent new governance techniques from falling capture. This is the internal critique.

For it to work the way it is supposed to, compliance-based governance assumes that regulators' toolkit and expertise are insufficient.[51] A traditional regulator might use a command-and-control approach where the state can ban products outright, place limits on behaviors, and hold industry accountable through court orders and litigated claims.[52] But a compliance-based model where industry is responsible for its own ongoing monitoring suggests this approach is ineffectual and limited. The private sector, proponents say, has technical expertise that government does not.[53] A command-and-control approach also raises a "pacing problem" where top-down regulation cannot keep up with fast-changing technologies. Therefore, compliance-based governance purports to bring "private sector expertise in[to] governance." It is also supposed to bring new enforcement mechanisms to regulators' command-and-control toolkit of rules and government enforcement agents.[54] The compliance model implies that if toolkits were sufficient, there would be no need for the nimbleness, flexibility, and speed, not to mention the input and exper-

---

[51]   Margot Kaminski, *Binary Governance: Lessons from the GDPR's Approach to Algorithmic Accountability*, 92 So. CAL. L. REV. 1529, 1564 (2019) (noting that collaborative governance adds "soft" law mechanisms like negotiated settlements, legal safe harbors, and incorporation of industry standards to traditional regulatory modalities).

[52]   *E.g.*, David A. Dana, *The New "Contractarian" Paradigm in Environmental Regulation*, 2000 U. ILL. L. REV. 35, 44–51 (comparing command-and-control to a site-specific negotiated form of governance).

[53]   Kaminski, *supra* note 51, at 1560.

[54]   *Id.* at 1560–62.

tise from private industry, that compliance-based governance brings to the information economy.

Compliance-based practices—impact assessments, compliance structures, self-audits and self-assessments, codes of conduct, industry self-certification, settlements, and consultations—are performative because they construct regulatory institutions that require those practices. The expectation that industry will bring its own experts to the table disincentivizes the government from funding the FTC's own experts. If regulated entities are hiring assessors and conducting audits by executive attestation on their own, the FTC does not need its own army of auditors and monitors to do the same job. And if most cases settle, Congress has an excuse to withhold the funding and staffing the FTC might need to litigate more claims. By making industry a partner in regulation, the compliance model explicitly and intentionally redistributes regulatory duties, relieving government of burdens but also normalizing the idea that government does not and should not have to perform traditional regulatory responsibilities. Industry is there to help.

Many other legal institutions are transforming themselves in the image of the compliance model. Industry input is engrained in modern environmental, health, and safety law.[55] Financial regulation in the wake of the 2008 Financial Crisis relies on audits, independent committees, and other internal structures that amount to outsourcing regulation to regulated entities themselves.[56] Compliance-based regulation and managerializa-

---

[55]   *See* DOUGLAS KYSAR, REGULATING FROM NOWHERE 100-5 (2010). *See also* Martha C. Nussbaum, *The Costs of Tragedy: Some Moral Limits of Cost-Benefit Analysis*, 29 J. LEGAL STUD. 1005, 1029-30 (2000); Amartya Sen, *The Discipline of Cost-Benefit Analysis*, 29 J. LEGAL STUD. 931, 936 (2000); Thomas O. McGarity, *The Goals of Environmental Legislation*, 31 BOSTON COLLEGE ENV. AFF. L. REV. 529, 551 (2004) (describing the Risk Assessment and Cost-Benefit Act of 1995, which would have required cost-benefit analysis in all regulatory programs); Cary Coglianese, *The Managerial Turn in Environmental Policy*, 17 N.Y.U. ENVTL. L. J. 54, 55-60 (2008) (describing managerialism in environmental law).

[56]   Rory Van Loo, *The New Gatekeepers: Private Firms As Public Enforcers*, 106 VA. L. REV. 467, 485-86 (2020) (demonstrating how CFPB regulators outsource regulation of third parties to banks); Rory Van Loo, *Regulatory Monitors: Policing Firms in the Compliance Era*, 119 COLUM. L. REV. 369, 397-98 (2019) (describing the role of internal compliance departments in financial regulation as a form of "collaborative governance").

tion have similarly expanded the importance of employer-friendly arbitration and played a crucial role in justifying forced arbitration clauses in employment contracts.[57] And, as we have discussed at length in this and in previous chapters, Lauren Edelman has shown how the corporate practices associated with Title VII—policy statements, diversity offices, bias training, and internal appeals—have performatively constructed what courts perceive anti-discrimination law to be.[58]

Scholars have argued that this kind of hollowing out of traditional regulatory functions is the product of neoliberal hegemony.[59] That is undoubtedly true. Procedural governance in environmental, health, and financial regulation law may also reflect the performativity of compliance practices on the ground. Put another way, we have come to expect that regulation is a public-private partnership in which industry manages much of its own compliance. Therefore, the compliance model has created legal institutions in its own image.

But this erosion of public institutional power undermines the very mechanisms that are supposed to help compliance-based governance guard against its own devolution into regulatory capture and self-regulation. As the compliance model's proponents concede, compliance-based governance is subject to the risk of capture, because regulated companies themselves are creating compliance tools and participating in their own regulation.[60] Accordingly, effective governance presupposes the existence of a robust and effective regulator that is capable and prepared to act as a "backdrop threat" to ensure that industry is an honest partner as it works with public institutions to achieve social goals.[61] But, as noted above, one of the performative aspects of the model is the construction of

---

[57]   Judith Resnick, *Diffusing Disputes: The Public in the Private of Arbitration, the Private in Courts, and the Erasure of Rights*, 124 YALE L.J. 2804, 2836-47 (2015).

[58]   EDELMAN, *supra* note 1, at 13.

[59]   Jedediah Britton-Purdy, David Singh Grewal, Amy Kapczynski and K. Sabeel Rahman, *Building a Law-and-Political-Economy Framework: Beyond the Twentieth-Century Synthesis*, 129 YALE L.J. 1796-1800, 1801-13 (2020).

[60]   Orly Lobel, *The Renew Deal: The Fall of Regulation and the Rise of Governance in Contemporary Legal Thought*, 89 MINN. L. REV. 342, 385 (2004) (conceding that collaborative governance tools may be "used by management merely as mechanisms for monitoring, controlling, and exerting additional pressures on workers").

[61]   Kaminski, *supra* note 51, at 1561.

public regulatory institutions that depend on industry expertise, input, capital, and workers to fulfill regulatory responsibilities. This dependence not only creates managerialized public institutions, but it also weakens the ability of government regulators to adequately function as enforcers ready to bring down the hammer of command-and-control if industry's compliance programs fail to rein in data-extractive practices.

However, the prospect of tethered regulatory agencies is far more likely than proponents suggest. When scholars describe the compliance model's diverse toolkit—from impact assessments to trainings and audits—they again make the epistemic error of considering the toolkit in a vacuum, divorced from the social context in which that toolkit is used. But compliance practices are not theories; they operate within organizational bureaucracies created to routinize productivity and profit.[62] Those bureaucracies can subordinate privacy structures to undermine accountability in any number of ways. Many companies push their CPO down the corporate hierarchy or subordinate them within risk management or compliance departments, forcing privacy to fight within systems focused on achieving substantially different goals.[63] Companies also shift control of privacy budgets to legal, compliance, or technology departments.[64] They also sideline privacy work. In self-reported surveys, privacy leaders report the greatest control over trainings, drafting policies, publications, communications, and travel, but far less responsibility for the things that really matter in compliance-based governance: audits, data inventory, and technology.[65] Management also creates siloed privacy departments

---

[62]   ARI EZRA WALDMAN, INDUSTRY UNBOUND: THE INSIDE STORY OF PRIVACY, DATA, AND CORPORATE POWER 210-31 (2021).

[63]   *Id.* at 144-48; IAPP, BENCHMARKING PRIVACY MANAGEMENT AND INVESTMENTS OF THE FORTUNE 1000: REPORT ON FINDINGS FROM 2014 RESEARCH (2014), https://iapp.org/media/pdf/resource_center/2014_Benchmarking_Report.pdf (showing that Fortune 1000 privacy leaders ranked "compliance" as the most important priority for the company).

[64]   *Id.* (finding that 80 percent of privacy budgets are spent on salaries, legal counsel, software, and overhead, whereas other budget items like incident response, privacy-related monitoring, and privacy-related investigations only comprise only 1–2 percent each of the remainder). *See also* Andrew Inkpen and Eric Tsang, *Social Capital, Networks, and Knowledge Transfer*, 30 ACAD. MGMT. REV. 146, 147-150 (2005) (demonstrating that budget shifting can undermine a corporate department's authority).

[65]   IAPP, *supra* note 63, at 5, 23.

that appear robust, but have little impact on the company's work.[66] Therefore, privacy law's reliance on privacy professionals—even those who consider themselves privacy advocates—doing work in the public interest is misplaced. Companies are already exercising their financial and structural power to co-opt internal privacy advocates and turn their efforts away from meaningful privacy work.[67]

The information industry also routinely fires dissident employees, creating a chilling effect on others trying to push against the data-extractive tide. In August 2020, for example, Buzzfeed reported that Facebook punished a senior engineer for collecting evidence showing the company gave preferential treatment to conservative accounts. Another Facebook employee who gathered evidence that the social network protected right-wing websites from the company's policies on misinformation had their internal access revoked, as well.[68] Google took the same approach to its employees who blew the whistle on the company's efforts to suppress unionization, its cozy relationship with outside advisers with long histories of homophobic and racist comments, and its entanglement with Customs and Border Protection.[69] Google even fired the prominent AI researcher Timnit Gebru for trying to publish a paper on language algorithms that threatened the company's bottom line.[70] This job insecurity has a chilling effect on tech-sector managers, dissuading them from speaking privacy truths to data-extractive power.

Any one of these constraints—weakened privacy offices, precarity of employment, and siloization, alone or in concert—weaken privacy law.

---

[66] Ari Ezra Waldman, *Designing Without Privacy*, 55 HOUSTON L. REV. 659, 709-719 (2018).

[67] WALDMAN, *supra* note 62, at 210–31.

[68] Craig Silverman and Ryan Mac, *Facebook Fired An Employee Who Collected Evidence of Right-Wing Pages Getting Preferential Treatment*, BUZZFEED NEWS (Aug. 6, 2020), https://www.buzzfeednews.com/article/craigsilverman/facebook-zuckerberg-what-if-trump-disputes-election-results.

[69] Noam Scheiber and Kate Conger, *The Great Google Revolt*, N.Y. TIMES (Feb. 18, 2020), https://www.nytimes.com/interactive/2020/02/18/magazine/google-revolt.html.

[70] Cade Metz and Daisuke Wakabayashi, *Google Researcher Says She Was Fired Over Paper Highlighting Bias in A.I.*, N.Y. TIMES (Dec. 3, 2020), https://www.nytimes.com/2020/12/03/technology/google-researcher-timnit-gebru.html.

Privacy departments that are siloed, starved for cash, and organizationally subservient to business units with independent or contrary interests have weaker voices in making policy. When advocates for accountability are fired, others may go silent. As a result, corporate obligations are framed in terms dictated by more powerful organizational actors, whether that is the general counsel, whose job it is to minimize legal risks to the company, or the vice president for technology, whose job it is to define the technical aspects of corporate practice. Neither of these actors is necessarily an active and overt anti-privacy voice. But the perspectives, goals, and metrics on which they are judged by their company are orthogonal to privacy and far more managerial. This makes it more likely that internal compliance practices will be framed and cabined to serve corporate interests rather than social and policy goals.

This creates a downward spiral. Compliance governance practices construct hollowed out regulatory institutions by normalizing the expectation that industry will fill in gaps left open by underfunded, slow-moving, and untrained public regulators. At the same time, it relies on internal corporate structures that are not independent of industry, but rather entirely controlled and subordinated by industry bureaucracies that can easily game the system. In this world, there are no honest partners and no backdrop threats. There is only self-regulation and symbolic compliance.

6.6   Conclusion

There is not much left about the second wave to be excited about after these critiques. The second wave of privacy law in the U.S. will serve industry at the same time it puts on a show of public governance. In a way, that is worse than the woefully inadequate first wave, which was never intended to regulate or constrain industry at all. The first wave was open and obvious about its biases; even the FTC, the very regulators supposed to protect consumers from predatory data-extractive corporations, wanted to protect a burgeoning Internet industry at all costs. But the second wave is different. It takes on the discourses and appearances of regulation without actually constraining industry from doing anything. And that will happen even if second wave laws are at their best. That is, even if companies within the information industry conduct their audits, complete impact assessments, keep records, hire new privacy professionals, train all employees on protecting privacy, and add privacy to their list of commitments to consumers, nothing stops them from expanding a business model premised on manipulation, extraction, and surveillance.

Maybe the second wave never wanted to do that. But it was certainly sold to us—and its proponents continue to maintain—that these proposals and new laws are strict, difficult for companies to comply with, will stifle innovation, and even end the Internet as we know it. None of that is true. The second wave is a gift to industry, and perhaps an even grander gift than the hands-off approach of the first wave.

Of course, this raises an obvious question: What's the alternative? In other words, if we are going to critique the first and second waves as inadequately addressing the power dynamics of informational capitalism, what could? What must be in privacy law's third wave? I begin to sketch out some third wave principles in the next Part.

PART III

PRIVACY LAW'S THIRD WAVE

7 Alternatives to the first and second waves

It should be clear by now that we need a third wave for privacy law in the United States. The first wave chose self-regulation, which almost never works. The second wave made some of the same mistakes as the first, but it also went further toward entrenching data-extractive practices. New individual rights (that few can exercise and have no effect on data-extractive capitalism) and new internal compliance requirements (which have turned into mere symbols of compliance) doubled down on privacy self-management while giving the information industry the gift of procedural compliance to legitimize its privacy invasive business model. The second wave may be different, but it isn't different in the ways we need.

Luckily, we are already seeing hints of new approaches. Some scholars have proposed treating data collectors as trustees or fiduciaries of our interests. Others have called for, and some legislators have proposed, civil rights and anti-discrimination approaches to privacy law. Still others seek even bigger interventions, including nothing short of how government and business function. In this Part, I will argue that we need to radically reimagine privacy law practices, forms of governance, and ideologies. First wave practices were based on notice, largely self-regulatory, and reflected classical liberalism; second wave practices were based on compliance, largely managerial, and reflected neoliberalism. What should the third wave look like? I think we need to mix the old and the new. We need to reclaim some tools of regulation that have been eclipsed by the compliance model. We also need to envision new alternatives to the managerial turn and, in particular, alternatives that reduce the mischief making powers of compliance departments or bypass them altogether. We need to think primarily about marginalized populations and those who bear the greatest risks in a surveillance economy. None of the current proposals for new privacy law meet all of those requirements. Perhaps we should think bigger. In this chapter, I discuss what privacy law could look like if we move beyond the managerialism and individual rights of the second wave.

A moderate approach might try to strike an acceptable balance between privacy and the monetization of data. A more radical approach might begin from the premise that the data-extractive, behavioral advertising-based business model of informational capitalism is structurally invasive, abusive, and subordinating, and therefore requires wholesale regulation and change. This chapter briefly outlines what either approach might look like. That the political environment today may not be ripe for more radical proposals is no reason to give up; it is instead the strongest rationale possible for framing a more robust alternative right now: We need to move the politically acceptable range of policies before it's too late.

A moderate approach could significantly boost funding for the FTC to create and enforce regulations.[1] The FTC and the Department of Justice could become more aggressive at enforcing anticompetition law so that individuals can obtain real power to choose between companies depending on their privacy practices. The FTC could require regular audits of all companies to ensure database accuracy, with annual reporting requirements and substantial punishments for failure. To regulate algorithmic decision-making systems that use vast amounts of data to make predictive, probabilistic decisions about people, the FTC could write a rule mandating a "minimum level of quality" in algorithmic decisions.[2] Some scholars have proposed a right to restitution from the ill-gotten gains from data collected by manipulative or misleading practices.[3] Data minimization—the notion that companies should only be allowed to collect and retain data that is absolutely necessary to achieve a previously defined and disclosed purpose—could be aggressively enforced.

These are just a few examples of a moderate approach to regulating data use in the information economy. They are, however, reformist. Reformist

---

[1] The FTC is trying to do just that. See Trade Regulation Rule on Commercial Surveillance and Data Security, 87 Fed. Reg. 51273 (Aug. 22, 2022) (to be codified at 16 C.F.R. ch. I).

[2] Daniel J. Solove, *The Limitations of Privacy Rights*, 98 NOTRE DAME L. REV. 975 (2023).

[3] *Id.* at 36.

reforms tweak institutions while maintaining capitalistic structures of power. A more radical approach—what André Gorz called "non-reformist reforms"—might target that business model directly. They leave intact an underlying labor- and data-extractive business model that subordinates every participant in the digital economy. Non-reformist reforms require a "modification of the relations of power," in particular "the creation of new centers of democratic power."[4]

7.1   What are non-reformist reforms

Gorz saw non-reformist reforms as a way to build a better world today while preparing for the world we want tomorrow. Reforms are "non-reformist" when they help bring about radical change.[5] Popular social movements could wait for structures of oppression to collapse under their own contradictions, shying away from incremental reforms within current systems of power for fear of legitimizing the systems and delaying real social transformation. Or, they could build both better lives and greater consciousness for the people along the way to structural change. Non-reformist reforms do the latter.

Amna Akbar's three essential characteristics of non-reformist reforms explain how to achieve this better world.[6] First, non-reformist reforms are never end goals; they are means to a transformative future. They are based not on a technocrat's assessment of what industry or those in power think is possible under the current regime. Rather, non-reformist reforms are meant to take us closer to what should be possible. Second, non-reformist reforms are always pathways for "building ever-growing organized popular power." This is as much about process as it is about substance. Non-reformist reforms come from social movements fighting for them rather than being meted out by those in power. The latter strengthens the

---

[4]   ANDRÉ GORZ, STRATEGY FOR LABOR 8, 8 n.3 (Martin A. Nicolaus & Victoria Ortiz trans., 1967).

[5]   Mark Engler and Paul Engler, *André Gorz's Non-Reformist Reforms Show How We Can Transform the World Today*, JACOBIN MAG. (July 22, 2021), https://www.jacobinmag.com/2021/07/andre-gorz-non-reformist-reforms -revolution-political-theory.

[6]   Amna Akbar, *Demands for a Democratic Political Economy*, 134 HARV. L. REV. F. 90, 112-17 (2020).

system that disenfranchises social movements and ordinary people, while the former recenters power. Finally, non-reformist reforms are never singular answers to discrete policy questions. They always aim at building popular power and, therefore, are part of a "broader array of strategies ... for political, economic, [and] social transformation." Non-reformist reforms are about "deepening consciousness, building independent power and membership, and expanding demands" all at the same time. They are not about targeting a single issue at the expense of other social demands, values, and visions.[7]

Consider a pay raise for union workers. A reformist reform is a raise granted by management, at their behest and by their largesse; a non-reformist reform is a raise won through struggle, protest, and activism, a process that awakens workers to their own power. A reformist reform is a raise that results when raises, however high, are the workers' ultimate goal; a non-reformist reform is a raise that opens the door for more demands, more struggles against power, and greater consciousness among workers of the system's subordination of workers generally. And a reformist reform is a raise that stands on its own; a non-reformist reform, by contrast, is a raise that is part of a larger ecosystem of structural change aimed at empowering workers. Let's apply these lessons to imagine what a third wave of U.S. privacy law might look like.

7.2   Privacy discourses

The theory of privacy-as-control embedded in the rights/compliance model maintains current structures of power. That is, although it seems empowering to be told that we should have control over when, how, and to whom we disclose our information, the reality is darker. As we have seen, continuing our reliance on individual privacy rights lulls us into a false sense of control while technology companies weaponize our exercise of individual rights to immunize themselves from legal accountability. Therefore, if we want to change the status quo, we need to start thinking and talking about privacy in terms other than choice, autonomy, and control. Our discourses of privacy should prioritize social values over industry interests and raise popular consciousness in the process.

---

[7]   *Id.* at 115–18.

There is already a rich body of privacy scholarship eschewing the individual-focused discourses of control and choice. For example, some scholars talk about privacy in terms of loyalty.[8] This would have profound implications for law reform. If we thought about privacy in terms of trust and loyalty, we might think that data collectors and technology companies owe us the same kind of fiduciary duties of care that doctors, lawyers, and accountants owe us. Those professionals are allowed to earn money and profit, but they can't do so by harming us; they can and should use our information, but they must do so in our interests. The argument for applying at least some of those rules to technology companies that collect and use our data makes some sense. On an interpersonal level, we tend to share when we trust. That we entrust our data to these companies and do so because we expect them to behave according to our expectations suggests that a relationship framed by fiduciary rules of care would be line with our general understanding of disclosure.

Others argue that privacy is about the flow of information through and among social networks.[9] This, too, would change the law. As Lior Strahilevitz has argued, a social networks approach to privacy law would protect as private information disclosed in one context that would not reasonably be expected to spread to other contexts. In other words, we would be able to share some information with some people—or some websites—and not have that information used elsewhere.

Helen Nissenbaum has focused privacy around "context-relative informational norms" that "govern[] the flows of personal information" in distinct social contexts, such as education, health care, and politics.[10] Julie Cohen has offered an even more robust conception of privacy. She argues that "[p]rivacy ... protects the situated practices of boundary management through which the capacity for self-determination develops."[11] Under that definition, privacy is among the most basic foundations for living the good life. Neil Richards argues that "privacy is about the rules governing the extent to which human information is detected, collected,

---

[8]   Woodrow Hartzog and Neil Richards, *The Surprising Virtues of Data Loyalty*, 71 EMORY L.J. 985 (2022).

[9]   Lior Strahilevitz, *A Social Networks Theory of Privacy*, 72 U. CHI. L. REV. 919-988 (2005).

[10]   HELEN NISSENBAUM, PRIVACY IN CONTEXT: TECHNOLOGY, POLICY, AND THE INTEGRITY OF SOCIAL LIFE 141 (2010).

[11]   Julie Cohen, *What Privacy Is For*, 126 HARV. L. REV. 1904, 1905 (2013).

used, shared, and stored and how those activities can be used to affect our lives."[12]

But we can go further. Although these approaches to privacy are not centered solely on the individual and, therefore, do not perpetuate the idea that privacy is something we must govern ourselves, they are still agnostic as to ends. They set the groundwork and lay foundations, but they do not take sides on ongoing tensions in the information economy. Some privacy scholarship is taking this next step.

Danielle Citron has called for giving special weight to, and protection for, sexual privacy, pushing back against corporate surveillance of our sexuality, bodies, and intimate selves.[13] Her work takes an explicitly normative turn by elevating sexual privacy as far more worthy of legal protection than the profit-making whims of a company that thinks extracting data from intimate applications and pornography websites is the path to wealth. For sexual privacy, procedure is not enough. Instead, sexual privacy demands the protection as a civil right. Civil rights "are legal rights whose protection are essential for human beings to flourish, enjoy respect, and feel that they belong. They are moral rights deserving of priority: they can't be traded away or denied without a [very] good reason."[14] A civil rights approach to privacy means a "baseline protection[]" for everyone, where privacy is a "right *to* something ... that let us 'thrive and be social,' feel like we belong, and engage as citizens."[15] If we want to turn privacy into a means for securing the preconditions for a good life, that means privacy law would have to be much more than procedural rules of the game, especially when that game undermines our capacity for true flourishing. A civil right to privacy, intimate or otherwise, could turn the entire information economy on its head.

Virginia Eubanks calls for special attention to protecting the privacy of those on public assistance, in the child welfare system, and those who are unhoused.[16] Scott Skinner-Thompson argues that privacy law should

---

12   NEIL RICHARDS, WHY PRIVACY MATTERS 3 (2021).
13   DANIELLE KEATS CITRON, THE FIGHT FOR PRIVACY (2022); Danielle Keats Citron, *Sexual Privacy*, 128 YALE L.J. 1870 (2019).
14   CITRON, *supra* note 13, at xviii.
15   *Id.* at 108.
16   VIRGINIA EUBANKS, AUTOMATING INEQUALITY: HOW HIGH TECH TOOLS PROFILE, POLICE, AND PUNISH THE POOR (2018).

adopt an anti-subordination approach that would protect the rights of the most vulnerable.[17] And Khiara Bridges wants privacy law to address structural socioeconomic inequality.[18] Privacy, Bridges found, is really a right guaranteed to the wealthy and privileged. Single parents, individuals on public assistance, and many communities of color are routinely denied privacy—over their bodies and their choices—and any system of regulation that retains those inequalities is complicit in discrimination.

For these third wave privacy scholars, privacy as a necessary element of human flourishing, or the realization of the whole person, including our physical well-being, happiness, self-determination, and more.[19] We need to stop thinking and talking about privacy in terms of choice and control, full stop. By leveraging discourse of emancipation—which is well underway in legal academia—we can change baseline assumptions about what privacy is for.

What if scholars and advocates started talking about privacy almost exclusively in terms of emancipation? Privacy would then be more than just a set of rules or a series of processes or even a set of norms. Privacy is a state of freedom from overlapping forms of subordination: corporate, institutional, and social. Privacy's emancipatory capacities underly Professor Citron's call for sexual privacy, which would liberate women, LGBTQ+ people, and sexual minorities from oppressive social and institutional structures, if fully protected. After all, as Citron notes, "we are free only insofar as we can manage the boundaries around our bodies and intimate activities."[20] Emancipation sits at the center of Salomé Viljoen's call for democratizing data governance to liberate people from a system of datafication that enacts, reifies, and amplifies unjust and unequal social relations.[21] Scholars and advocates should adopt this language when speaking and thinking about privacy. Doing so will contribute to new ways of thinking about the role of privacy law, privacy litigation, and privacy wrongs.

---

[17] SCOTT SKINNER-THOMPSON, PRIVACY AT THE MARGINS (2020).
[18] KHIARA BRIDGES, THE POVERTY OF PRIVACY RIGHTS (2017).
[19] *See generally* MARTHA NUSSBAUM, CREATING CAPABILITIES: THE HUMAN DEVELOPMENT APPROACH (2011).
[20] Citron, *supra* note 13, at 1873.
[21] Salomé Viljoen, *A Relational Theory of Data Governance*, 131 Yale L.J. 573, 583 (2021).

7.3   Power and policy

New discourses are important, but they only begin a process of countering privacy law's pro-industry performances. We should think about the kind of privacy performances we want in terms of power: to whom do they allocate power, from whom do they take power, and against whom is the law weaponized? To date, privacy law discourses and behaviors have empowered industry to extract our data for profit with limited accountability. We can change that by reclaiming the regulatory ideal, more common during the post-World War II era, that government regulation acts on behalf of the people and as a counterweight to powerful industry bent on domination.

Redistributing power means regulators should think about their role differently. Jodi Short aptly notes that the last few decades of economic regulation in the U.S. reflects a "paranoid style."[22] The paranoid style of regulation is one in which regulators, the very people tasked with ensuring capitalists comply with the democratically developed rules that constrain their worst excesses, refuse to do their jobs. Rather than focusing on their social welfare missions, paranoid regulators are paralyzed by fear of doing too much, or stifling innovation, of getting too involved in the market. A product of neoliberal and conservative discourses about the role of government, the paranoid style is the do-nothing style. It is the style that prefers industry self-regulation or public-private partnerships because paranoid regulators don't actually believe that government can be a force for good.

Instead of partnering with industry, conceptualizing their regulatory role as industry partners, and occasionally requiring companies to pay compensatory fines, regulators must recognize that the data-extractive harms caused by industry are metastatic.[23] For example, Amazon agreed to pay $61.7 million in a settlement with the FTC, a number derived from adding up the precise amounts of tips the company stole from its delivery

---

[22]   Jodi Short, *The Paranoid Style in Regulatory Reform*, 63 Hastings L. J. 633, 635 (2012).

[23]   Paul Ohm, *Regulating at Scale*, 2 Geo. L. Tech. Rev. 546, 546-47 (2018) (arguing that the exponential scale of some harms requires an approach different from linear regulation).

drivers over two years.[24] At less than 0.015 percent of the company's revenue in a single year, the fine is neither likely to have any material effect on Amazon nor deter future mischief. But the harm Amazon caused to workers exceeds the lost compensation. Amazon's growth and profit stem from a business model that places impossible demands on underpaid workers while maintaining strict surveillance of worker life. Amazon workers cannot leave their posts to use the restroom; the company pays particularly low wages. An investigation into Amazon's employment practices demonstrated that the company engages in a series of tactics, like siphoning tips, not simply to nickel-and-dime workers, but to encourage employees to leave, keeping wages down. Surveillance keeps employees afraid. Stealing tips is part of a patchwork of strategies subordinating workers.[25]

Data processing harms also metastasize for users. The FTC fined Facebook $5 billion for its role in the Cambridge Analytica scandal, but it has had little effect. Individual users were subject to manipulation by Cambridge Analytica because of how social networks function, the lack of regulation over what it means to "consent" to terms of service, and the capacity of data processing to create relational harms. Facebook's fine was accompanied by marginal changes in what third-party apps can do, but the company has not changed the underlying data processing mechanisms that subjected millions of users to Cambridge Analytica's data misuse.[26]

Instead of slaps on the wrist, the Department of Justice (DOJ) should be empowered to hold industry executives personally liable when they lie or mislead regulators in corporate privacy assessments. In terms of new regulatory practices, many privacy advocates, and at least one former FTC Commissioner, have called on the FTC to litigate claims more often.[27] Congress must also empower the FTC to pursue more robust

---

[24]   In the Matter of Amazon.com, Inc., File No. 1923123 (F.T.C. Feb 2, 2021) (Agreement Containing Consent Order).

[25]   David Leonhardt, *The Amazon Customers Don't See*, N.Y. TIMES (June 15, 2021), https://www.nytimes.com/2021/06/15/briefing/amazon-warehouse -investigation.html.

[26]   Nilay Patel, *Facebook's $5 Billion FTC Fine is an Embarrassing Joke*, THE VERGE (July 12, 2019), https://www.theverge.com/2019/7/12/20692524/ facebook-five-billion-ftc-fine-embarrassing-joke.

[27]   Dissenting Statement of Commissioner Rohit Chopra, at 7, Regarding Zoom Video Communications, Inc., F.T.C. File No. 1923167 (F.T.C. Nov.

remedies, including disgorgement, to deter wrongful conduct by forcing defendants to give up profits derived from their illegal behavior. And not just disgorgement of the profits, but also any algorithms derived from the data and, of course, the data itself. Amazon did not just steal $61.7 million from its drivers; it also derived enormous profits from a booming delivery market during the COVID-19 pandemic in which it underpaid its workers while promising otherwise. A percentage of customers likely used Amazon services based on that promise.

Since disgorgement of ill-gotten profits may have a stronger effect on corporate behavior, a similar model could rein in data misuse. Indeed, disgorgement need not only apply to money. Data collection feeds algorithmic processes that target individuals with advertisements; behavioral targeting, in fact, is at the core of the Internet business model. If microtargeting algorithms are the products of improper data collection, then the algorithms themselves are ill-gotten gains, and should be similarly disgorged. FTC Commissioner Rebecca Slaughter has already hinted that this would be a welcome shift in regulators' practices.[28]

We must also redistribute power away from the information industry by facilitating critical research about data-extractive technologies. Making radical changes in trade secrecy laws is an obvious first step. At least one scholar has argued that private technology companies seeking to do business with the government through procurement should have to give up their trade secrecy rights for the privilege (and enormous revenue) that come with government contracts for automated decision-making systems.[29] Another scholar argues that we need a private version of the Freedom of Information Act and a trans-substantive information commission to implement robust public and private data transparency so civil society, classes of plaintiffs, and independent academics can see precisely

---

6, 2020), https://www.ftc.gov/system/files/documents/public_statements/1582914/final_commissioner_chopra_dissenting_statement_on_zoom.pdf.

[28] Rebecca Slaughter, Protecting Consumer Privacy in a Time of Crisis, Remarks of Acting Chairwoman Rebecca Kelly Slaughter 2, Future of Privacy Forum (Feb. 10, 2021), https://www.ftc.gov/public-statements/2021/02/remarks-commissioner-rebecca-kelly-slaughter-future-privacy-forum.

[29] Hannah Bloch-Wehba, A Public Technology Option, 86 L. & CONTEMP. PROBS. (forthcoming 2023).

what companies are doing with our data.[30] Policymakers and regulators need to look beyond cynically performative transparency via privacy policies and vague reports and demand full transparency of the underlying data used for everything from behavioral targeting to content moderation administration.

Given industry's current monopoly over the raw data necessary to assess technology's social effects, the mass unionization of technology researchers employed by industry can shift power to those seeking to pull back the veil on corporate misdeeds. Google's summary firing of Timnit Gebru suggests that corporate-funded information research is not independent.[31] In Gebru's situation, a union could have acted as a check against retaliation, discrimination, or forcing internal technology researchers to "strike a positive tone" in their work.[32] Organized and empowered employees could push back on corporate development of technologies that harm marginalized populations. The rights/compliance model assumes that in-house compliance and privacy professionals will play the role of the privacy advocate. That is unlikely, given ordinary workplace pressures facing in-house compliance professionals.[33] A union for technology workers doing important research on information economy harms may help. In the spirit of non-reformist performances, the activism and struggles of unionization can also awaken technology company workers to their exploitation within organizational structures and their role in designing products explicitly aimed at extracting data and profits from subordinated consumers.

---

[30]   Margaret Kwoka, *Scoping an Information Commission*, 86 L. & CONTEMP. PROBS. (forthcoming 2023).

[31]   Karen Hao, *We Read the Paper that Forced Timnit Gebru Out of Google. Here's What It Says.*, MIT TECH. REV. (Dec. 4, 2020), https://www .technologyreview.com/2020/12/04/1013294/google-ai-ethics-research -paper-forced-out-timnit-gebru/.

[32]   Paresh Dave and Jeffrey Dastin, *Google Told Its Scientists to 'Strike a Positive Tone' in AI Research—Documents*, REUTERS (Dec. 23, 2020), https://www.reuters.com/article/us-alphabet-google-research-focus/google -told-its-scientists-to-strike-a-positive-tone-in-ai-research-documents -idUSKBN28X1CB.

[33]   Lauren Edelman et al., *Legal Ambiguity and the Politics of Compliance: Affirmative Action Officers' Dilemma*, 13 L. & POL'Y 73, 78 (1991).

The rights/compliance model of governance provides "rules of the game" without committing companies or society to any particular ends.[34] A radically different approach would base privacy law on the principle of justice, or the basic notion that information systems should not create or entrench "social subordination."[35] That can start with changing how we make privacy law.

Today, regulators and policymakers seek industry input. They should instead give advocacy organizations representing marginalized populations, and not corporations, a seat at the table. Groups focused on the cyber civil rights of women, the poor, communities of color, victims of intimate partner violence and nonconsensual pornography, sex workers, those living with disabilities, HIV+ individuals, and those who identify as LGBTQ+, among many others, may have unique perspectives on data use, its dangers, and downstream consequences. Those most likely to be subordinated by data practices should be in the room; those most likely to subordinate others should not be. They may not always agree or have a single message, but they certainly have claims to seats at the table that are currently given to industry by default.

One of the results of decentering the needs of industry in privacy law is an emphasis on cyber civil rights. Ohio Senator Sherrod Brown's bill, the Data Accountability and Transparency Act (DATA) of 2020, comes closest among recent proposals to doing this. Although the draft bill retains some of the rights/compliance framework, it creates an office of civil rights that would ensure data collection and use is "fair, equitable, and nondiscriminatory."[36] The proposal would prohibit any data aggregation that results in discrimination in housing, employment, credit, insurance, and public accommodations or that has a disparate impact on marginalized populations.[37] It also makes it easier for victims to prove, and obtain justice for, disparate impact. Of course, DATA is not immune

---

[34]   Meg Leta Jones and Margot E. Kaminski, *An American's Guide to the GDPR*, 98 Denv. L. Rev. 93, 108, 110 (2020).

[35]   Jedediah Britton-Purdy, David Singh Grewal, Amy Kapczynski and K. Sabeel Rahman, *Building a Law-and-Political-Economy Framework: Beyond the Twentieth-Century Synthesis*, 129 YALE L.J. 1796-1800, 1824 (2020).

[36]   Data Accountability and Transparency Act, S. __, 116th Cong. (2020), at §301(b)(1).

[37]   *Id.* at §104 (shifting the burden of proof to the data aggregator to show absence of discrimination or other alternatives to discrimination).

from any of the problems of the second wave. But non-reformist reforms are consciously imperfect. DATA nods to the population-level harms that are endemic to business models dependent upon data-driven behavioral targeting. It is worth noting that in drafting his proposal, Senator Brown consulted exclusively with representatives of civil society and not with industry.[38] Senator Brown's decision to focus on equality rather than on what corporations would accept is a welcome model for new privacy performances.

Frank Pasquale also has a provocative proposal for "ex ante licensing of large-scale data collection ... in jurisdictions committed to enabling democratic governance of personal data."[39] Pasquale proposes a stricter version of Senator Brown's DATA that would require data brokers to obtain a license from the government in order to process large data sets of personal information. This proposal sounds radical, but the notion that some information is too sensitive to use for business purposes is commonplace. For instance, we criminalize the dissemination of a person's bank account information, and universities require researchers to obtain approval before engaging in any human-subject research. In other words, we place limits on gathering and sharing information about real people all the time because we are concerned about both the downstream effects and social values that are lost if we did not. Pasquale argues that an ex-ante licensing regime would be the only way to protect the population, particularly the most marginalized, from "systematic efforts to typecast individuals, to keep them monitored in their place, or to ransack databases for ways to manipulate them."[40] This proposal already has a solid foundation in other areas of U.S. law. The financial law scholar Saule Omarova has proposed mandatory ex-ante approval of financial products; Andrew Tutt has proposed something similar for algorithms.[41] Managerialized

---

[38] Brown Releases New Proposal That Would Protect Consumers' Privacy From Bad Actors, https://www.brown.senate.gov/newsroom/press/release/brown-proposal-protect-consumers-privacy; Statements by Privacy Experts and Civil Rights and Consumer Organizations.

[39] Frank Pasquale, *Licensure as Data Governance*, KNIGHT FIRST AMEND. INST. (Sept. 28, 2021), https://knightcolumbia.org/content/licensure-as-data-governance.

[40] *Id.*

[41] Saule Omarova, *License to Deal: Mandatory Approval of Complex Financial Products*, 90 WASH. UNIV. L. REV. 63, 63 (2012); Andrew Tutt, *An FDA for Algorithms*, 69 ADMIN. L. REV. 83 (2017).

compliance cannot protect individuals from harm, nor does it even try. It is content with managing data collection and trying to regulate it ex post, after it is used and after it likely has already had an effect on social life.

Ultimately, though, the best way to protect privacy in the information economy is to provide a robust alternative to a digital environment premised on surveillance-for-profit. A public option as an alternative to for-profit data extractive platforms—like Medicare is a public option for health insurance—may be the only way to chip away at what seems like a pre-determined march toward a society and economy of total surveillance. Alongside government, educational institutions and nonprofits can create public, private-protective options for web browsing (like FireFox), instant messaging (like Signal), and even mobile dating apps. We can still do all the things the data-extractive economy offers us. We just need to provide the world with options that do not collect, share, and process their data for profit.

7.4 Making privacy decisions

In the first and second waves, corporate decisions about how (or how not, more likely) to integrate privacy into design were almost entirely unregulated. To be sure, the GDPR includes a requirement of "data protection by design and by default," but as we have seen, that law largely envisions data protection as a set of procedures that manage or surround data collection, sharing, and use. So when the GDPR talks about design and default, it means making internal structures of compliance part of the fabric of the design process. As I have argued, that's not nearly good enough.

Because they are unregulated, privacy decisions inside the information industry follow cost-benefit analysis, a core managerial impulse.[42] Privacy protective steps are taken only if their costs do not materially undermine or limit short-, medium-, and long-term revenue outlooks. Julie Cohen argues that cost-benefit analysis "rest[s] on sets of assumptions about how to describe, measure, and account for program costs and benefits. Those assumptions are neither transparent nor inherently neutral, and merit

---

[42] Ari Ezra Waldman, Industry Unbound: The Inside Story of Privacy, Data, and Corporate Power (2021).

careful scrutiny based on both the values that they enshrine and those that they elide or omit."[43]

Cost-benefit analysis for privacy has several problems. The decision-making process lends itself easily to fuzzy, manipulative math. That is, it is easy to calculate the benefits of disclosure—they are often proximate in time, immediately tangible to individual users, and quantifiable in terms of efficiency gains. But the costs are harder to calculate; privacy risks may only materialize in the future and although they may be substantial then, present-day cost-benefit calculators with industry profits on their minds can easily shrink the present discounted value of future harms they think are hypothetical. More profoundly, cost-benefit analysis for privacy design is also premised on the resolute certainty that all components of a privacy design decision can be reduced to numbers. Frank Pasquale rightly argues that this is an epistemic weakness of cost-benefit analysis wherever it is used: Even if we could agree on the questions to ask, the notion that we can always and with certainty assign a determinate value to all things (like privacy risks) is utter fantastical and, to be frank, arrogant.[44] Is there a certain monetary value to clean air? Is there a certain monetary value to the nourishment and flourishing that comes from privacy protection?

Rather than simply requiring companies to complete an impact assessment—a process routinely reduced to perfunctory box-checking—the law can instead require certain types of privacy decision-making processes. Instead of thinking about raw costs and benefits, scenario analysis would force companies to consider the worst harms to individuals and consumers, bringing the needs of the most marginalized populations into privacy and product design.[45] It is at this stage that companies should be

---

[43]   Julie E. Cohen, Between Truth and Power: Legal Constructions of Informational Capitalism 194 (2019). See also Frank Ackerman and Lisa Heinzerling, Priceless: On Knowing the Price of Everything and the Value of Nothing (2004); Douglas A. Kysar, Regulating from Nowhere: Environmental Law and the Search for Objectivity (2010); Matthew D. Adler, Incommensurability and Cost-Benefit Analysis, 146 U. PENN. L. REV. 1371 (1998).

[44]   Frank Pasquale, Power and Knowledge in Policy Evaluation: From Managing Budgets to Analyzing Scenarios, 86 L. & CONTEMP. PROBS. (forthcoming 2023).

[45]   Id.

required to consider outsider input, input from marginalized populations in particular. There is no shortage of models for knowledge production that prioritize the needs of those most likely to be harmed by this or that policy. To date, however, privacy law has assumed that introducing new kinds of knowledge production and sensemaking practices isn't its job. It is. And the third wave should invite it.

7.5 Conclusion

Civil rights. Strong punishments. The rejuvenation of the public regulator. New modes of thinking about privacy. Considering the needs of the most marginalized. Public options. These principles mark just the beginning of what privacy law's third wave might look like. We are still figuring that out. Hopefully, this short book has highlighted both the need for a third wave and its foundational premises. It is now up to us—students, scholars, practitioners, and anyone interested in privacy—to make policymakers listen, to make real change, and to bring us closer to a better world where information platforms facilitate human flourishing rather than destroy it.

8   Conclusions on U.S. Data Privacy Law

By framing privacy law in the United States as a series of waves, we can see beyond them, to a future horizon of possibility. We can replace self-regulation and the managerial turn with public accountability. We can replace privacy-as-choice and privacy-as-control with privacy-as-a-human-right. We can, if we have the will, replace data-extraction with data-empowerment. The question, then, is this: How do we build this movement?

In that regard, informational capitalism has an advantage over industrial capitalism. The harms of the latter were ultimately visible (although only after a long effort from activists, many of whom were women and workers of color): illness and death from diseased meat that was sold to consumers in the absence of food safety regulations, abject poverty stemming from the lack of worker protections and a minimum wage, working women jumping to their deaths out of a burning factory because government never imposed any workplace safety regulations, black soot and smoke hovering in the air over industrial cities because there were no rules protecting the environment from industrial capitalism's endless pursuits of profit.[1] Journalists, scholars, and activists identified these and other

---

[1]   These examples come from the most famous incidents and investigations into the harms of the industrial revolution in the United States. *See, e.g.*, UPTON SINCLAIR, THE JUNGLE (1906) (contaminated beef); JACOB RIIS, HOW THE OTHER HALF LIVES (1890) (poverty in the slums of the Lower East Side of New York City); EDVIGE GIUNTA AND MARY ANNE TRASCIATTI, TALKING TO GIRLS: INTIMATE AND POLITICAL ESSAYS ON THE TRIANGLE SHIRTWAIST FACTORY FIRE (2022) (Triangle Shirtwaist Factory fire); STEPHEN MOSLEY, THE CHIMNEY OF THE WORLD: A HISTORY OF SMOKE POLLUTION IN VICTORIAN AND EDWARDIAN MANCHESTER (2d ed. 2008) (air pollution in urban areas).

excesses of industrial capitalism. The harms of informational capitalism are there, but as yet, they are less proximate, less graphic, and less obvious. It is, therefore, harder to build an active, ground-up social movement to push for the kind of real structural change that we need.

But we are not without hope. If we think about privacy as a civil right that enables all of us, especially most marginalized, to flourish, then privacy should be part of the missions of every single civil rights organization on the map. From Lambda Legal, Gay and Lesbian Advocates and Defenders, and the Human Rights Campaign (organizations committed to protecting the rights of queer people) to the NAACP and the NAACP Legal Defense Fund (organizations dedicated to Black civil rights) to any similarly situated organization advocating on behalf of the civil rights of people of color and other minoritized groups, each organization can play a role in building a privacy social movement. Of course, these organizations should focus on ensuring equal treatment of oppressed people. But protecting their privacy is part of what equal treatment means. Look no further than organizations like the STOP LAPD Spying Coalition, a group of local activists who have experienced police over-surveillance and police brutality and who are now organizing members of their community to push back against an oppressive surveillance state. Our goal should be to take that model and apply it to surveillance capitalism.

We know from experience, not to mention the works of scholars like Anita Allen, Khiara Bridges, Scott Skinner-Thompson, and Danielle Keats Citron, that privacy is most often a right of the privileged. Black women, poor women, queer people, and all sexual and gender minorities have the least amount of privacy for various structural reasons. Activist groups and non-profit advocacy organizations dedicated to serving these communities have a responsibility to update their missions and expand their work to include protecting privacy of their community members as part of their civil rights. Once we start thinking about privacy alongside equality, justice, and emancipation, a social movement for reform may just be possible. A third wave for privacy law will follow.

Bibliography

Acquisiti, Alessandro, Leslie K. John, and George Loewenstein. 2012. "The Impact of Relative Standards on the Propensity to Disclose." *Journal of Marketing Research* 49: 160–174.

Acquisti, Alessandro and Jens Grossklags. 2008. "What Can Behavioral Economics Teach Us About Privacy." In *Digital Privacy: Theory, Technologies, and Practices* 363–374. Edited by Alessandro Acquisti et al. London: Auerbach Publications.

Adjerid, Idris, Alessandro Acquisti, Laura Brandimarte, and George Loewenstein. 2013. "Sleights of Privacy: Framing, Disclosures, and the Limits of Transparency." *SOUPS '13: Proceedings of the 9th Symposium on Usable Privacy and Security.*

Allen, Anita L. 1988. *Uneasy Access: Privacy for Women in a Free Society.* New York: Rowman & Littlefield Publishers.

Allen, Anita L. 2000. "Gender and Privacy in Cyberspace." *Stanford Law Review* 52: 1175–1200.

Allen, Anita L. 2010. "Privacy Torts: Unreliable Remedies for LGBT Plaintiffs." *California Law Review* 98: 1711–1764.

Bamberger, Kenneth A. and Deirdre K. Mulligan. 2011. "New Governance, Chief Privacy Officers, and the Corporate Management of Information Privacy in the United States: An Initial Inquiry." *Law and Policy* 33: 477–508.

Bamberger, Kenneth A. and Deirdre Mulligan. 2015. *Privacy on the Ground: Driving Corporate Behavior in the United States and Europe.* Cambridge, MA: The MIT Press.

Barocas, Solon and Andrew D. Selbst. 2016. "Big Data's Disparate Impact." *California Law Review* 104: 671–732.

Benjamin, Ruha. 2019. *Race After Technology: Abolitionist Tools for the New Jim Code.* New York: Polity.

Bradford, Anu. 2012. "The Brussels Effect." *Northwestern University Law Review* 107: 1–68.

Bridges, Khiara. 2017. *The Poverty of Privacy Rights.* Palo Alto, CA: Stanford University Press.

Britton-Purdy, Jedediah David Singh Grewal, Amy Kapczynski, and K. Sabeel Rahman. 2020. "Building a Law-and-Political-Economy Framework: Beyond the Twentieth-Century Synthesis." *Yale Law Journal* 129: 1796–1835.

Butler, Paul D. 2013. "Poor People Lose: *Gideon* and the Critique of Rights." *Yale Law Journal* 122: 2176–2204.

Chander, Anupam, Margot E. Kaminski, and William McGeveran. 2021. "Catalyzing Privacy Law." *Minnesota Law Review* 105: 1733–1802.

Citron, Danielle Keats and Benjamin Wittes. "The Internet Will Not Break: Denying Bad Samaritans § 230 Immunity." *Fordham Law Review* 86: 401–423.

Citron, Danielle Keats and Daniel J. Solove. 2022. "Privacy Harms." *Boston University Law Review* 102: 793–863.

Citron, Danielle Keats and Frank Pasquale. 2014. "The Scored Society: Due Process for Automated Predictions." *Washington Law Review* 89: 1–33.

Citron, Danielle Keats and Mary Anne Franks. 2014. "Criminalizing Revenge Porn." *Wake Forest Law Review* 49: 345–391.

Citron, Danielle Keats. "Sexual Privacy." *Yale Law Journal* 128: 1870–1960.

Citron, Danielle Keats. 2009. "Cyber Civil Rights." *Boston University Law Review* 89: 61–125.

Citron, Danielle Keats. 2009. "Law's Expressive Value in Combating Cyber Gender Harassment." *Michigan Law Review* 108: 373–415.

Citron, Danielle Keats. 2021. "A New Compact for Sexual Privacy." *William and Mary Law Review* 62: 1763–1839.

Citron, Danielle Keats. 2022. *The Fight for Privacy: Protecting Dignity, Identity, and Love in the Digital Age.* New York: W. W. Norton.

Cohen, Jean L. 2001. "The Necessity of Privacy." *Social Research* 68: 318–326.

Cohen, Julie E. 2013. "What Privacy Is For." *Harvard Law Review* 126: 1904–1933.

Cohen, Julie E. 2019. "Turning Privacy Inside Out." *Theoretical Inquiries in Law* 20: 1–31.

Cohen, Julie E. 2019. *Between Truth and Power: Legal Constructions of Informational Capitalism.* New York: Oxford University Press.

Cohen, Julie E. and Ari Ezra Waldman. 2023. "Forward: Framing Regulatory Managerialism as an Object of Study and Strategic Displacement." *Law and Contemporary Problems* 86 (forthcoming).

Cranor, Lorrie F. 2012. "Necessary but not Sufficient: Standardized Mechanisms for Privacy Notice and Choice." *Journal of Telecommunications and High Technology Law* 10: 273–308.

Draper, Nora and Joseph Turow. 2019. "The Corporate Cultivation of Digital Resignation." *New Media and Society* 21: 1824–1839.

Edelman, Lauren, Stephen Petterson, Elizabeth Chambliss, and Howard S. Erlanger. 1991. "Legal Ambiguity and the Politics of Compliance: Affirmative Action Officers' Dilemma." *Law and Policy* 13: 73–97.

Edelman, Lauren. 2016. *Working Law: Courts, Corporations, and Symbolic Civil Rights.* Chicago, IL: University of Chicago Press.

Eubanks, Virginia. 2018. *Automating Inequality: How High Tech Tools Profile, Police, and Punish The Poor.* New York: Macmillan.

Flanigan, Mary and Helen Nissenbaum. 2016. *Values at Play in Digital Games.* Cambridge, MA: The MIT Press.

Fried, Charles. 1968. "Privacy." *Yale Law Journal* 77: 475–493.

Gray, Megan. 2018. "Understanding and Improving Privacy 'Audits' Under FTC Orders." *Stanford Law School Center for Information and Society.*

Grewal, David Singh and Jedediah Purdy. 2014. "Introduction: Law and Neoliberalism." *Law and Contemporary Problems* 77: 1–23.

Hargittai, Eszter and Alice Marwick. 2016. "What Can I Really Do? Explaining the Privacy Paradox with Online Apathy." *International Journal of Communications* 10: 3737–3757.

Hartzog, Woodrow and Daniel J. Solove. "The Scope and Potential of FTC Data Protection." *George Washington Law Review* 83: 2230–2300.

Hartzog, Woodrow and Neil Richards. 2020. "Privacy's Constitutional Moment and the Limits of Data Protection." *Boston College Law Review* 61: 1687–1762.

Hartzog, Woodrow. 2018. *Privacy's Blueprint: The Battle to Control the Design of New Technologies.* Cambridge, MA: Harvard University Press.

Harvey, David. 2007. "Neoliberalism as Creative Destruction." *Annals of the American Academy of Political and Social Science* 610: 21–44.

Hoofnagle, Christopher Jay. 2016. *Federal Trade Commission Privacy Law and Policy.* New York: Cambridge University Press.

John, Leslie K., Alessandro Acquisti, and George Loewenstein. 2011. "Strangers on a Plane: Context-Dependent Willingness to Divulge Sensitive Information." *Journal of Consumer Research* 37: 858–873.

Jones, Meg Leta and Margot E. Kaminski. 2020. "An American's Guide to the GDPR." *Denver Law Review* 98: 93–128.

Kahneman, Daniel. 2011. *Thinking, Fast and Slow.* New York: Farrar, Straus, and Giroux.

Kaminski, Margot E. 2019. "Binary Governance: Lessons from the GDPR's Approach to Algorithmic Accountability." *Southern California Law Review* 92: 1529–1616.

Kaminski, Margot E. 2022. "The Case for Data Privacy Rights (or, Please, a Little Optimism)." *Notre Dame Law Review Reflection* 97: 385–399.

Katyal, Sonia K. 2019. "Private Accountability in the Age of Artificial Intelligence." *University of California, Los Angeles Law Review* 66: 54–141.

Lobel, Orly. 2004. "The Renew Deal: The Fall of Regulation and the Rise of Governance in Contemporary Legal Thought." *Minnesota Law Review* 89: 342–470.

Marwick, Alice and Eszter Hargittai. 2018. "Nothing to Hide, Nothing to Lose? Incentives and Disincentives to Sharing Information With Institutions Online." *Information, Communications, and Society* 22: 1697–1713.

Mathur, Arunesh, Gunes Acar, Michael J. Friedman, Eli Lucherini, Jonathan Mayer, Marshini Chetty, and Arvind Narayanan. 2019. "Dark Patterns at Scale: Findings from a Crawl of 11K Shopping Websites." *Proceedings of the ACM on Human-Computer Interaction.*

McDonald, Aleecia M. and Lorrie F. Cranor. 2008. "The Cost of Reading Privacy Policies." *I/S: A Journal of Law and Policy for the Information Society* 4: 543–568.

Milne, George R. and Mary J. Culnan. 2004. "Strategies for Reducing Online Privacy Risks: Why Consumers Read (or Don't Read) Online Privacy Policies." *Journal of Interactive Marketing* 18: 15–29.

Nelson, Robert L. and Laura Beth Nielsen. 2000. "Cops, Counsel, and Entrepreneurs: Constructing the Role of Inside Counsel in Large Corporations." *Law and Society Review* 34: 457–494.

Nissenbaum, Helen. 2010. *Privacy in Context: Technology, Policy, and the Integrity of Social Life.* Palo Alto, CA: Stanford University Press.

Noble, Safiya. 2018. *Algorithms of Oppression: How Search Engines Reinforce Racism*. New York: New York University Press.

Norberg, Patricia A., Daniel R. Horne, and David A. Horne. 2007. "The Privacy Paradox: Personal Information Disclosure Intentions Versus Behavior." *Journal of Consumer Affairs* 41: 100–126.

Norman, Donald. 1988. *The Design of Everyday Things*. New York: Basic Books.

Nussbaum, Martha. 2011. *Creating Capabilities: The Human Development Approach*: Cambridge, MA: Harvard University Press.

Ohm, Paul. 2018. "Regulating at Scale." *Georgetown Law and Technology Review* 2: 546–556.

Posner, Richard. 1978. "The Right of Privacy." *Georgia Law Review* 12: 393–422.

Reidenberg, Joel R. 2014. "Disagreeable Privacy Policies: Mismatches Between Meaning and Users' Understanding." *Berkeley Technology Law Journal* 30: 39–88.

Reidenberg, Joel R. 1999. "Restoring Americans' Privacy in Electronic Commerce." *Berkeley Technology Law Journal* 14: 771–792.

Reidenberg, Joel R., N. Cameron Russell, Alexander J. Callen, Sophia Qasir, and Thomas B. Norton. 2015. "Privacy Harms and the Effectiveness of the Notice and Choice Framework." *I/S: Journal of Law and Policy for the Information Society* 11: 485–524.

Resnick, Judith. 2015. "Diffusing Disputes: The Public in the Private of Arbitration, the Private in Courts, and the Erasure of Rights." *Yale Law Journal* 124: 2804–2939.

Richards, Neil M. 2010. "The Puzzle of Brandeis, Privacy, and Speech." *Vanderbilt Law Review* 63: 1295–1354.

Richards, Neil M. 2021. *Why Privacy Matters*. New York: Oxford University Press.

Richards, Neil M. and Woodrow Hartzog. 2019. "The Pathologies of Digital Consent." *Washington University Law Review* 96: 1461–1503.

Richardson, Rashida, Jason Shultz, and Kate Crawford. 2019. "Dirty Data, Bad Predictions: How Civil Rights Violations Impact Police Data, Predictive Policing Systems, and Justice." *New York University Law Review* 94: 192–233.

Samuelson, William and Richard Zeckhauser. 1988. "Status Quo Bias in Decision Making." *Journal of Risk and Uncertainty* 1: 7–59.

Scheibehenne, Benjamin, Rainer Greifeneder, and Peter M. Todd. 2010. "Can There Ever Be Too Many Options? A Meta-Analytic Review of Choice Overload." *Journal of Consumer Research* 37: 409–425.

Short, Jodi L. 2012. "The Paranoid Style in Regulatory Reform." *Hastings Law Journal* 63: 633–694.

Skinner-Thompson, Scott. 2020. *Privacy at the Margins*. New York: Cambridge University Press.

Solove, Daniel J. 2004. *The Digital Person: Technology and Privacy in the Information Age*. New York: New York University Press.

Solove, Daniel J. 2008. *Understanding Privacy*. Cambridge, MA: Harvard University Press.

Solove, Daniel J. 2013. "Introduction: Privacy Self-Management and the Consent Dilemma." *Harvard Law Review* 126: 1880–1903.

Solove, Daniel J. 2021. "The Myth of the Privacy Paradox." *George Washington Law Review* 89: 1–51.

Solove, Daniel J. and Danielle Keats Citron. 2018. "Risk and Anxiety: A Theory of Data-Breach Harms." *Texas Law Review* 96: 737–786.

Solove, Daniel J. and Woodrow Hartzog. 2011. "The FTC and the New Common Law of Privacy." *Columbia Law Review* 114: 583–676.

Solow-Niederman, Alicia. 2022. "Information Privacy and the Inference Economy." *Northwestern University Law Review* 117: 357–424.

Strahilevitz, Lior. 2005. "A Social Networks Theory of Privacy." *University of Chicago Law Review* 72: 919–988.

Turow, Joseph, Yphtach Lelkes, Norah Draper, and Ari Ezra Waldman. 2023. "Americans Can't Consent to Companies' Use of Their Data." *Annenberg School of Communications, University of Pennsylvania.*

Tushnet, Mark. 1993. "The Critique of Rights." *Southern Methodist University Law Review* 47: 23.

Vaidhyanathan, Siva. 2011. *The Googlization Of Everything (And Why We Should Worry).* Berkeley, CA: University of California Press.

Vaidhyanathan, Siva. 2018. *Anti-Social Media: How Facebook Disconnects Us and Undermines Democracy.* New York: Oxford University Press.

Van Loo, Rory. 2019. "Regulatory Monitors: Policing Firms in the Compliance Era." *Columbia Law Review* 119: 369–444.

Van Loo, Rory. 2020. "The New Gatekeepers: Private Firms As Public Enforcers." *Virginia Law Review* 106: 467–522.

Viljoen, Salomé. 2021. "A Relational Theory of Data Governance." *Yale Law Journal* 131: 573–654.

Waldman, Ari Ezra and James A. Mourey. 2020. "Past the Privacy Paradox: The Important of Privacy Changes as a Function of Control and Complexity." *Journal of the Association of Consumer Research* 5: 162–180.

Waldman, Ari Ezra. 2018. "Designing Without Privacy." *Houston Law Review* 55: 659–727.

Waldman, Ari Ezra. 2018. *Privacy As Trust: Information Privacy for an Information Age.* New York: Cambridge University Press.

Waldman, Ari Ezra. 2020. "Cognitive Biases, Dark Patterns, and the 'Privacy Paradox'." *Current Opinions in Psychology* 31: 105–109.

Waldman, Ari Ezra. 2020. "Privacy Law's False Promise." *Washington University Law Review* 97: 773–834.

Waldman, Ari Ezra. 2021. "Outsourcing Privacy." *Notre Dame Law Review Reflection* 96: 194–210.

Waldman, Ari Ezra. 2021. "The New Privacy Law." *University of California, Davis Law Review Online* 55: 19–42.

Waldman, Ari Ezra. 2021. *Industry Unbound: The Inside Story of Privacy, Data, and Corporate Power.* New York: Cambridge University Press.

Waldman, Ari Ezra. 2022. "Privacy, Practice, and Performance." *California Law Review* 110: 1221–1280.

Waldman, Ari Ezra. 2022. "Privacy's Rights Trap." *Northwestern University Law Review* 117: 88–106.

Warren, Samuel D. and Louis D. Brandeis. 1890. "The Right to Privacy." *Harvard Law Review* 4: 193–220.

Westin, Alan F. 1967. *Privacy and Freedom*. New York: Ig Publishing.

Wexler, Rebecca. 2018. "Life, Liberty, and Trade Secrets: Intellectual Property in the Criminal Justice System." *Stanford Law Review* 70: 1343–1429.

Index

American Data Protection and Privacy
  Act 60
antitrust enforcement 31
artificial intelligence 3, 56
audits 2, 4, 8, 42, 44, 49, 52, 77–8, 86,
  94
automated decision-making 40, 102
autonomy 18–19, 21–2, 23, 27, 49,
  58, 96

balance of power, in informational
  capitalism 7
behavioral advertising 102–5
  collection of data for 5, 34, 94
binary governance 39
biometric information, collection and
  use of 35
'bottle bill' referendums, in California
  and Colorado 65
Brandeis, Louis 11
Brookings Institution, The 50
Brussels Effect 46
Butler, Paul 67–8

California Consumer Privacy Act
  (CCPA) 39, 47, 52, 60
California's Online Privacy Protection
  Act (CalOPPA) 17
Cambridge Analytica 101
Campbell v. St. John 34
Cardozo, Benjamin 19
Chhabria, Vince 34
chief privacy officers (CPOs) 4, 41, 73
Children's Online Privacy Protection
  Act (COPPA) 1
choice architecture 29

Citron, Danielle 98
Civil Rights Act, Title VII of 72
civil rights law, corporate compliance
  with 72–3
climate change 65, 68
codes of conduct 4, 44, 48, 52, 86
Cohen, Jean 21, 37
Cohen, Julie 106
collaborative governance 2, 43–4, 71
commodification and corporate
  surveillance 6
common law of torts 11
compliance 41–5, 47, 51–2, 70, 72–4,
  83
comprehension at scale, illusion of
  24–7
consent
  power of 40
  to sell customer data 40
cost-benefit analysis 50
  anti-regulatory logics of 72
Cranor, Lorrie Faith 24
critique of rights 67
customer data, consent to sell 40
cyber civil rights 104

dark patterns, in platform design 33,
  59
Data Accountability and Transparency
  Act (DATA) 40, 104
data collection 33, 40, 102
  for behavioral advertising 34
  at scale 25
  in surveillance economy 26
  types of digital information
    collected by companies 26

Titles in the **Elgar Advanced Introductions** series include:

International Political Economy
Benjamin J. Cohen

The Austrian School of Economics
Randall G. Holcombe

Cultural Economics
Ruth Towse

Law and Development
Michael J. Trebilcock and Mariana Mota Prado

International Humanitarian Law
Robert Kolb

International Trade Law
Michael J. Trebilcock

Post Keynesian Economics
J.E. King

International Intellectual Property
Susy Frankel and Daniel J. Gervais

Public Management and Administration
Christopher Pollitt

Organised Crime
Leslie Holmes

Nationalism
Liah Greenfeld

Social Policy
Daniel Béland and Rianne Mahon

Globalisation
Jonathan Michie

Entrepreneurial Finance
Hans Landström

International Conflict and Security Law
Nigel D. White

Comparative Constitutional Law
Mark Tushnet

International Human Rights Law
Dinah L. Shelton

Entrepreneurship
Robert D. Hisrich

International Tax Law
Reuven S. Avi-Yonah

Public Policy
B. Guy Peters

The Law of International Organizations
Jan Klabbers

International Environmental Law
Ellen Hey

International Sales Law
Clayton P. Gillette

Corporate Venturing
Robert D. Hisrich

Public Choice
Randall G. Holcombe

Private Law
Jan M. Smits

Consumer Behavior Analysis
Gordon Foxall

Behavioral Economics
John F. Tomer